Finding My Mammy!

by

John Thomas Keating, MA

authorHOUSE™

1663 LIBERTY DRIVE, SUITE 200
BLOOMINGTON, INDIANA 47403
(800) 839-8640
WWW.AUTHORHOUSE.COM

First published by AuthorHouse 12/13/05

ISBN: 1-4208-7651-1 (sc)

Printed in the United States of America
Bloomington, Indiana

This book is printed on acid-free paper.

Table of Contents

PREFACE

America is the Great Melting Pot of the World according to many pundits. That's not necessarily so! Picture a salad bowl. There are various types of lettuce, sliced cucumbers and carrots, perhaps celery, maybe a diced radish or two, some like apple bits, others raisins, tomatoes, and croutons. All of this mixture is covered with any number of delectable dressings. A salad is not a bowl of dead, melted fruits and vegetables. Each segment has a distinct flavor and texture that adds to the mixture. What would a salad be without tomatoes, or lettuce? Got the Gestalt on that one? Sorry, my therapist side is showing.

Gestalt is a form of Psychology where *perception* is the key to understanding. Piecing the parts of one's life together gets you a Gestalt – or enlightenment as to what you are, as you "sense" it. The sum is truly greater than all of its parts. So, the Gestalt on this salad thing is many different flavors joined together that make for a delightful addition to the main course of meat and potatoes. In allegorical terms, meat and potatoes equals perhaps law and order with a side of various subcultures that we take for granted in our greater culture called "American." There is one more ingredient that makes the salad sing - the dressing. Let's call it freedom. It affects all the meal! The problem with the dressing is this: It usually does not reach every bit of the salad. Those on top get its covering first, and then it trickles down and may very well smother whatever is lying on the bottom of the bowl. It's called decadence.

Too much of anything can kill you! The amount of dressing is determined by one's desire to pour it on. That desire may be controlled by a generous, or tightly clinched hand. Let's call the hand equality, shall we?

There is a problem with the hand though. It's connected to an arm, a shoulder, then neck, and finally, the head! The head watches the salad and decides what it will taste like using its tongue that is very particular. It can be conditioned to get used to more freedom, or less, depending upon need. The head need is **survival** where all historical and traditional perceptions originate. If the tongue isn't conditioned, it may deprive the salad of its full flavor, or not enough, which in turn is accepted or rejected by the head. The head may sense something is wrong and make appropriate adjustments, usually. Of course, the head has life experiences of its own. It's a tricky process. Let's call this process the Great Experiment – the United States of America! How's that for a Gestalt?

This book is about one man's experiences *in* several different segments of the salad called America. From the get go, you will discover that *my head* loves all segments equally! Although, there may be moments when you find yourself weeping, then laughing and probably being in shock don't put your salad fork down! The tears I have shed at first were because of my own realization of just how deprived I *thought* I had been. But, as my Chinese brothers and sisters so aptly put it – I learned to "cry happy"! We're going deep into the whys and what fors that most people would like to know, but are too ashamed to ask about. The topic of sex may come up. After all, that is how we all got here! There are myths, and then there's reality – how some segments of the salad have directly, or indirectly, affected even the intimate practices of other salad members will be discussed!

One more ingredient that I personally enjoy goes on top of the salad – shredded cheese! In this case, let us call the cheese more love from my heart to yours than you can possibly imagine! That's where I'm coming from! The Bible says, "Perfect love casts out all fear!" So, lets take the smaller, outside fork. We gently grasp it and very lightly use the tongs to feel the textures of what we will discover is a beautiful mixture that tickles, teases, sours, sweetens and bitters our collective tongue in the process of breaking spiritual bread together.

One more thing, I freely admit that my skin tone is decidedly white – well, actually more of the light tan variety. However, my ancestry is not as pure as my appearance suggests. ***I discovered that there is an African connection to the vast majority of Irish people, which is my ancestral lineage.*** My name is John Thomas Keating. The family, or clan, name goes back as long as anyone can remember in the Land with no Snakes! Saint Patrick drove them out generations earlier, so the story goes. My clan origin is a place called in the Gaelic language "Ianskeaton," or the Falls of Keating according to an Irish Roman Catholic Priest I had interviewed for a paper in multicultural studies while attending Prairie View A & M University year's prior. From time to time, you will receive history, sociology, psychology, domestic violence, anger management, drug and alcohol and race-relations lessons that may feel painful, but that's were the healing is – in the pain. I can speak with authority on the matter as a retired Counselor. So, here we go my dear brothers and sisters. Please understand some of the names of characters in the book have been changed to protect them from certain harm. Remember that I LOVE YOU, however JESUS LOVES YOU MORE! He *is* the **Master Salad Maker**!

John Thomas Keating, MA

Definitions

Race: A competitive event; an antiquated term that identifies the physical characteristics that are all too often used by others to discriminate, oppress, subjugate or commit genocide against.

Racism: The deliberate misuse of power, be it economic or otherwise, by one ethnic group to subjugate, control or eliminate another ethnic group.

Economic Racism: The deliberate usage of monetary wealth to entrap and subjugate one ethnic group by the perceived superior ethnic group.

Unaware Racism: Attitudes and beliefs that one is superior and has automatic privilege over others because of racial stereotyping without realizing it.

Institutionalized Racism: Attitudes, beliefs and practices whereby one person, or group of persons, is implied superior over others because of racial stereotyping within all fields of endeavor be it legal, educational, corporate entities, public or private industries.

Stereotyping: Automatically identifying persons as being a specific way; or assuming that a person looks a specific way, before investigating that person for one's self.

Depersonalizing: The deliberate act of taking away the individuality of a person, or group of persons, with the end result of seeing them as objects – not people.

Objectifying: Seeing any person, or persons, as being less than human and more like a machine.

Genocide: The deliberately planned elimination of persons simply because they might be different in any way, shape or fashion.

Apartheid: The deliberately planned and executed separation of one ethnic group from others usually based on the attitude that the one is superior to the others.

De Facto: Anything, or law, that exists that is not necessarily written down - they are implied.

Segregation: The deliberately planned partial separation of one ethnic group from other ethnic groups usually based on the attitude that one group is superior over the others.

Miscegenation: The antiquated idea/laws based on a multiracial concept that one-person cannot/should not marry, co-habitat or mix with other races especially if progeny are probable.

Privilege: The concept based on superiority that one race has the right to excel, or be first at/in anything over other racial groups.

Black: The inclusion of all the colors of the spectrum; also, a global view based on oppression, apartheid and genocidal experiences having the end result of mental torture, paranoia, and/or stress leading to diseases or early death; having a "bunker mentality."

White: The absence of any color from the spectrum; also, an attitude of superiority with specific attached behaviors that lead to the exclusion of other ethnic groups if at all possible, or by any means necessary.

Prejudice: A pre-decided view or position concerning any idea, person or thing especially when it comes to race relations.

Bigotry: A close-minded world-view whereby others are automatically excluded usually based on rationalization, justification and/or intellectualization.

Hate: A reactionary emotion constituting fear of any person, place, thing or situation.

Nazism: Pseudo religious cult practice with its base being the belief that white people are superior in every way over other ethnicities.

Bonding: The process by which persons emotionally attach themselves to other people, places, things or situations.

Chapter One
The Circle's Beginning

Writing a book is a tricky thing. It is exhilarating at times, acutely painful at others, disheartening and tedious. It is a process of emotionally "dumping" what the author believes is his, or her, truth. It is not easy! Hours upon hours are spent just sitting and deliberating over perhaps one word, and how it will affect what is being portrayed. Writing is much like the artist who uses paint and brush upon a canvas to express his, or her, personal vision, interpretation or message. Words are the paint of the writer. His, or her, brush is either a typewriter or computer. The canvas is paper that is copyrighted, submitted to a publisher, and if he, or she, is very fortunate, published and disseminated broadly. So, if you are reading this book then that means I have been most fortunate indeed! Let's get down to the story, shall we?

St. James Church dominates two corners in the Midtown District of near central Houston, Texas. It was begun way back in nineteen seventeen by a small group of devoted church ladies. Their epidermal complexion was decidedly much lighter then, than the present occupants of enthusiastic in-your-face African Americans whose experiences lay in oppression, discrimination, de facto apartheid and historical genocide. There are a few European Americans – white folks - who may venture in on a temporary basis, perhaps, and then move on. They come more out of curiosity than brotherhood. My story is a bit different than your usual "white bread" that arrived with an air of unrealized superiority and arrogance. In time, I found I could absolutely live without those defects of character! A female member who had taken a liking to me asked if I would at least check it out. I am not one to rush into anything. It took six months to finally enter the doors. I am so very grateful to God for her for inviting me; and, God loving me enough to help me be a member in the church.

My first Sunday service was just before Thanksgiving of 1995. What an experience! The people out front were packed in a serpentine like line, much like sardines ready for the eating from a can. Ever so gently, the herd of worshippers edged their way up the outer steps, through the anteroom and into the sanctuary. Oh my God, what a sight! A large arch graced the stage behind the enthusiastic choir. Antiquated pipes from another era of sedate organ accompanied worship still stood sternly erect filling the archway. The ceiling had large 4 by 8 sheets of painted plywood neatly bolted in place to cover the ill begotten holes. But, what caught my eye was located above the arch. Large golden colored letters stretched across just below the ceiling. They proclaimed **Jesus Is Lord.** I swear as God is my judge, they seemed to glimmer with fire as the choir hit up a more rapid and rhythmic version of "Pass Me Not Oh Gentle Savior" than I was use to. I felt right at home clapping my hands to the heavy down beat. A salty tear gently trickled down my left cheek. This church was *happening*!

This was not my first experience in an African American worship setting. I had recently left the largest "minority" Southern Baptist Convention church in the Greater Houston Area. It was above the national average for black socio-economic status. Attendance there was on a regular basis for me. I was met with resistance often by some members, and to my surprise, a few somewhat nervous "dates" from others. It had taken me about a month to figure out why some should be so stand-offish. I remembered what a Chinese Pentecostal minister had once said to me when he had asked a black minister to bring his church over on a Sunday afternoon to have a "get together." The Reverend said point blank, "Sunday is the only time of the week where we can get together and be **ourselves**. But, thank you very much for the invitation, Sir!" This short and forgetful four-eyed white boy had been intruding without realizing it, at first. I arrived at the SBC church because a member, who genuinely wanted to see The Dream live, had invited me. He wanted to see full integration of his church. He had kept saying to me in late night talks where we both worked, how the most segregated hour of the week is still eleven o'clock Sunday morning. He had come to know me as a friend, not the *white devil* that so many black folks call us surreptitiously. All of these thoughts, and more, raced through my mind as I allowed myself to go with the flow in that first Saint James experience.

A standing ritual at the church is to welcome new neighbors and everybody gets a hug. I rose on my size seven feet and found numerous hands stretching toward me. And yes, I did get hugs. I thought to myself how much I had missed by not allowing *me* earlier in life to find out for *myself* about other cultures. And yet, my entire existence has been a journey through several different cultures. I was blessed beyond my wildest imagination! I simply had not realized it yet. It would take nine more years before what had been planted in the garden of my mind's experiences would begin to bloom! The lady who invited me in the first place would eventually become my best friend in the whole wide world. The Minister, who once had such great misgivings about me, would eventually invite me back with open arms. I would be given a rainbow family full of rich stories both painful and delightful at the same time. In the twenty-third Psalm it says, "My cup runneth over. Surely goodness and mercy will follow me all the days of my life."

November 26th of 1946 was a banner day, if you happen to be me! I entered the world from the womb of a sixteen-year-old "Black-Irish" Ohio Buckeye girl who had no idea what motherhood was all about. Her husband had been drafted into the U.S. Army and was serving in Occupied Japan. This bouncing baby boy was given the name of John Lowell Thomas Stevens. I went home to a dingy house filled with mother's siblings that at best fought each other on a daily basis. My birth mother's name was Mabel. She fled the madness for bars and dance floors. Eventually, Ohio State Child Protective Services stepped in and plucked me out of that abusive environment. According to the newspaper, my case was one of the worst in state history! Mabel was found guilty of child neglect and abandonment. She served a year in the Marion, Ohio State Penitentiary for Women. I was remanded to kindly, middle-aged foster parents. My birth father returned to the United States to divorce Mabel and make arrangements for my adoption to my Great Uncle and his wife. My birth certificate was changed to reflect Everett and Mary Keating as my birth parents although the truth lay in a sealed file. So, I reverted back to my birth mother's maiden family name! My ancestral heritage was kept intact. Although I never met my birth father - Jessie, I am grateful that he made sure his son had a very proud Irish name and long heritage. Little would I realize that the fact that I never met my birth father would make me very useful in my adult years for helping others with similar background – especially African American males!

The young adoptive couple had moved from Muncie, Indiana to a small rural church near Oakwood, Ohio. They found that there was something very wrong with their "little Johnny." He would sit for hours not moving, or saying anything. It seemed that he always had some sort of illness including double pneumonia. Their son was diagnosed with possible Autism! The family doctor had more bad news. He stated that if their son were not moved to a warmer climate, he would probably die. His lungs were not fully developed. Plus, the abuse and starvation from his infant years left him sickly and often times near death. These young parents had an awesome task in front of them - keep alive a child seemingly marked for death from birth. They elected to take a small rural church near Colquitt, Miller County, Georgia in 1950.

Life was very difficult for Everett and Mary Keating adjusting to a southern, segregated lifestyle. To top it off, they were life long Republicans that made them stand out on election days like sore thumbs. The early fifties in Georgia saw the unholy alliance of the Dixie Democrats and the Ku Klux Klan. Jim Crow was the established order making sure that black folks stayed in their places at the bottom of the socio-economic ladder. Lynching was not unheard of; nor was rape! This was the environment that this young Christian couple from Springfield, Ohio was led to by God! And what of little Johnny? He learned lessons that would be his downfall and later salvation in his life! No one in that small family was exempt from what was to befall them.

Everett Charles Keating was a Godly man who was dedicated to Christ's purpose that no one should be lost into eternal damnation. His preaching style was somewhat low key. He rarely expressed emotion except for an occasional tear when he encountered someone else who was hurting. He had the gift of showing mercy. He stood five feet and eight inches. His eyes were a very dark blue and he had coarse straight jet-black hair. He had an olive complexion. By contrast, Mary Ruth stood five feet and three inches tall. She had light blue eyes and wavy blonde hair. It was almost like fine silk strands. She was temperamental and very controlling. He was cool and calm; she was seething with some sort of deep-seated rage. And little Johnny was caught in the middle. Years later, I learned that they had fought about adopting me. He wanted me and she did not. My very existence represented the one thing that she could not have – a child of her own. Little did I realize why the rage until it happened to me at age five and one-half by a white female caregiver! Sexual abuse. Need I say more? I think not because there is a God Who delivered me from that agony of shame held inside for decades, as the reader shall witness later on in this book. That abuse ultimately became one more asset in counseling others!

This small family moved from town to the county where two additions entered the Keating household. A brother and sister team became my foster big siblings. His name was Pleasant and hers was Walene. They were the product of a poor, abusive alcoholic white sharecropper. Both of them eventually moved on to colleges where they became professional persons. He became a high school teacher. She became a registered nurse. A pattern began to emerge in the life of little Johnny – a lack of permanence. Stability was nonexistent. Within the next two years, the family

moved twice again. The final residence in Miller County was
an abandoned sharecropper's house complete with back forty,
outhouse and barn for storing cotton before sale to the gin. Times
had gotten hard for the Keatings. Little Johnny found his small,
frail hands picking cotton at age six in the parching heat. He did
his best to keep up with the "darkies" as African Americans were
known back then. Little did he realize that two simultaneous
events would create an emotional conflict that only a Supernatural
Force could be able to solve? Love verses hate; ignorance verses
knowledge; and, good verses evil planted in one little boy. How on
earth would this turn out? God knew before he was born!

A new face appeared at the doorway of the old sharecropper's
home. She was about twenty-eight, slender, broad nose, thick lips
and one tooth missing up front. She wore a bandana over her dark,
curly hair. She was the next-door neighbor's common law wife.
Her name was Eula and she was very black! I shall never forget
when my adoptive mother introduced her to me. Keep in mind that
my parents were from "up north", and their global view of others
was decidedly different. Mother instructed Eula as to my care
and feeding. She then made a statement that turned my suspicion
into absolute terror! Her words to Eula sent chills down my spine.
"If Johnny should act up, you have my permission to spank his
behind!" That simply was never done by what were known as
Mammies in those days. Eula asked her to repeat the instruction
evidently not comprehending my adoptive mother's frame of
reference. The order was repeated. Eula said, "Yes, Mam." My
mother left for her music teaching position at the local elementary
school. I was left with a black female with equal authority to any
white person in Miller County, Georgia! Well, at least she was
equal in our house. The year was 1953!

That first year of elementary school was hell on earth. I hated
sitting in place and didn't mix well with any of my classmates. I
had already become a loner. My favorite past time was watching
the classroom clock tick on until the 3:00 PM bell sounded. It was
time to ride the big yellow bus home. I'd hop off the steps and
on to the dusty path that led to the front stoop where Eula would
be waiting for me patiently. Every morning, she would take this

make shift broom and go out front shouting, "Shoo! Shoo! Shoo!" She'd swing the broom violently and cry out to Jesus! She made me stand on the stoop while all this was going on. I watched with mild curiosity wondering why she went to all that trouble for me. What she was doing was driving snakes out of the front yard that had slithered up from the swamp behind the back forty. She took her job very seriously, so I figured. I was to learn years later, in 1995, the real reason she gave so much of herself to me.

Eula and I **bonded**. It became a ritual that was played out every day except Sunday. I'd come home and start running through the house. Eula would begin to chase me. Eventually, her dark, bony, and calloused fingers caught me. She would swoop me up in her arms and march me to a large wooden chair in the living room. I would be firmly situated on her lap. She began to sing Spirituals to me. In due time, my head would nod until it lay upon her chest. I could hear a very large and loving heart beating a rhythm that crossed an ocean and the ages. She became my security. In spite of the racism I was unknowingly learning in a segregated school system, a truly Christian lady had planted a counter seed of love. Who would have known just how powerful that seed would be in the years to come! Some say you cannot return home again. I beg to differ! To this day, when I hear black gospel, chills run up my spine. I have to clap my hands and tap my feet. Eula gave me the gift of love when it seemed no one else cared about a insignificant little white boy who lived with nightmares and shame.

Tom, Eula's husband came over now and then to say "howdy" and walk his woman home. He had this huge, lumbering mammal complete with mane and graying mussel. It was his mule. This beast of burden came in very handy when plowing time arrived to plant more cotton in the back forty. Much to my delight, Tom would firmly sit me on the old mule's back and make a few rounds. He would cautiously watch as I giggled with glee. Tom didn't want anything to happen to Johnny, not so much out of retribution from my parents, but because of Eula's insistence! She genuinely loved this little white boy. Although she was semi-literate – meaning she could sign her own name – she instinctively knew a deep hurt lay within my being. That's what the songs and embraces were for.

7

She provided a "soul medication" that was a blessed balm soothing my emotional pain.

My adoptive father's church had choir practice on Thursday nights. I sat next to my mother on the front pew entertaining myself with a pencil and paper. It seemed that I could draw almost any cartoon character there was. I had learned very early to turn inward not out of self-friendship, but because the outer world was too painful. Suddenly, there was a loud rap on the main church door. It was repeated! Father stopped his directing duties and went to see what might be the matter. His frame disappeared almost immediately outside. About five minutes passed, as everyone seemed to hold his or her collective breath. He re-appeared and came over to my mother. He bent over and said in a concerned voice, "There's been an incident. I'm going into town with Tom [Eula's husband]." He stopped long enough to ask the gathering to pray and left into the night's darkness.

Mother drove back to the house with uncharacteristic silence. She put me to bed and went to my parent's bedroom. I could hear her crying and praying. I knew something big had happened, but what? Time seemed to creep by. Eventually, Dad came home. I could hear them talking quietly. He said something about a white man, a black woman, her husband and a fireplace poker. The white man got away and came back with his buddies to whip on the black man for defending his woman's honor. They said he was taken to town for a "trial?" Tom got word of the goings on and came to ask my Dad to please make some sense out of the madness. To my Father's credit, he did stand up to the crazed gathering, but to no avail. The man was hung? My Dad came home broken hearted.

The next morning, I could feel the tension in the house. Eula didn't show up for work! Mom stayed home. Dad went over to the church for some books and returned. About 6:00 PM, a caravan of trucks and cars could be seen creating plumes of dust as they headed for our home. Dad told Mom to go to the bedroom and pray. I was pushed into a closet. Dad went out onto the front stoop and waited for the arrival of what must have seemed like an armada of red necked, straw hatted, pot bellied thugs. There were no sheets on this venture. One of them came up on the stoop. Dad stood silently. The man said, "Evening Preacher. Nice night isn't it?" Dad said nothing. The man continued, "You damned Yankees have gone too far this time! We didn't say nothing when your wife invited the niggers in for tea and played her accordion." He was referring to a gathering Mom had for Eula's birthday with her friends in escort for a party. We didn't say anything when you and your family went out picking cotton with **them**. But, God damn it, Preacher! When you get into business that ain't yours, we can't let that happen.

We ain't gonna kill you cause you are a minister. You're just another damn Yankee. You got one week to get the hell out of Miller County." I had gently pushed the closet door open to see as much as I could. My face disappeared behind the door again as Dad came back into the house looking very pale. I could see the reflection of yellow and orange coming from the front yard. The caravan left its calling card complete with the stench of burning kerosene and burlap wrapped around dried boards in the shape of a cross. I could hear my parents talking softly, but in rapid cadence. Both were upset. I lay in my bed wishing Eula were there. I needed a song and hug, but that was never to be again. She didn't return. A live chicken and a poke salad were left on the front stoop instead. I withdrew deep into myself. I was angry, but at my tender age, I didn't understand why. Some forty years later while studying for my Masters Degree in Counseling, I learned of the gut wrenching effects of abandonment issues, and how they can destroy the "self" if allowed to continue too long. No healthy relationship can be forged with the fear of being left behind lurking in the shadows. *Clinging too tight can drive the very object of one's affection away. It's called Enmeshment. The result is serious rejection or abandonment issues.*

Four days after the incident and the ensuing cross burning, the family moved northward to Albany, Georgia. I entered the second grade there. I felt so alone. My much older foster sister left for nurse's school in Atlanta. I struggled to maintain smiles to please others. My insides felt very much like ground meat. Both of my parents worked at that time. They deemed it necessary for me to become what is now known as a "latch key kid." I listened to the radio mostly. Evening serials like Sky King, Sergeant Preston of the Canadian Mounted Police and Rin Tin Tin helped me forget the tragic events played out that led to separation from the one person who seemed to understand me. I seemed not to care anymore about anything. I was only seven years of age and had experienced more than most adults face in their entire miserable, incepid existences.

Just when I began to come out of my shell and make a new friend, the family moved to the east side of Albany. Both my parents worked for the government at a local Marine base. I was placed in the care of a Mrs. Jackson. She was a kindly lady whose husband owned the house we lived in. It was located on Red Rock Road. Her two sons were about my age and we played incessantly. One of our favorite past times was sneaking into a nearby watermelon patch. We'd steal a melon and break it open. Yes, our fingers got sticky, but who cared as we slurped our way into full stomachs. I personally enjoyed the bright yellow meat melons the best!

Dad had gone to Atlanta to ostensibly see my foster sister, Walene. The Biggest Show on Earth had come to Albany. Mom took me to see the gala festivities. There were dozens of animal acts and numerous clowns. I remember asking Mom if it were true that elephants had long memories. She said, "Yes, they do! And, they are all Republicans too!" Years later, I admit I finally got what she meant. She was trying to be funny. Problem was, I seemed to have this inability to tell when people were either being serious or just joking. It's a part of another diagnosis I finally received under the expert care of a Psychologist: Major Depression. All this was tied to past experiences that were subconsciously clouding my thinking. Yes, I had school friends, but no one to really feel safe with enough to let down my guard around. ***Loneliness will bring on Depression if you allow it to continue unchecked for long enough.***

Red Rock Road became our family's last residence before returning to Ohio. My lungs had developed sufficiently in the South to warrant a bill of good health. I was coming up on my ninth year on planet earth. Our family had purchased its first television! Now I could see Rin Tin Tin, Sky King and other heroes. The TV became my closest friend. It seemed to have everything, and I didn't have to think. Thinking brought on pain. But, I learned that there were others who were experiencing pain for a vastly different reason than mine. There were civil rights demonstrations in a place called Montgomery, Alabama. Some black woman refused to go to the back of a city bus. There was this minister that had started a boycott, whatever that was. Keep in mind; I'm only eight years old. Little did I realize that in 1965, I would be in Montgomery, Alabama! I would receive a permanent scar from someone like those that burned a cross in Miller County, Georgia and caused my family's flight to Albany.

On my ninth birthday my Father had a big surprise for me. We drove to the local airport and Dad signed us in. He simply said, "Follow me, son." We walked on to the tarmac and there it was a Beechcraft V-Tail private plane. A man in sunglasses shook Dad's hand and he opened the door for us. Dad sat in the second row and I was riding "shot gun" right next to the pilot! We taxied out to the runway and we were off! The little plane gently rose and began to bank to the right. We were headed east. I stretched my neck to see as much of everything that I could. Suddenly, the pilot said, "Hold on!" He sharply banked the plane to the right again. I looked out the window and some 1000 feet below was Red Rock Road! The neighbors came out of their house to look up and find out why this little plane was circling overhead. It was the Jacksons! You better believe when we got home, I had a story to tell the kids next door! "That was me up there in the plane!" My fascination for aircraft would ultimately send me half way around the world where I would obtain still more scars.

My Father was very active in something secret toward the end of our time in the South. I remember seeing a long, old black car slowly drive by our home. The horn beeped and it moved onward down the road a short piece. Dad said he was going for a walk; he'd be back soon. The TV was on, but something inside of me said look out of the side living room window. Dad and three black men were talking near the old car. Finally, Dad returned to the house. He seemed dismayed as he said to my Mother, "There's going to be more trouble here." I mentally shrugged my spiritual shoulders and went back to the TV.

Soon after that meeting, our family returned to Springfield, Ohio. There's so much more that I could write about the South, but one thing I have learned in life: It's not so much about me and my exploits after all. It's all about what a loving God can do through me that really matters! All of my scars were a part of a Master Plan that is only now unfolding for others to consume much like that salad! ***God really does know everything! We do not have to. Our job is to trust and obey!***

Chapter Two
Rebel, Yankee, Nazi

The family moved northward back to our home roots. Dad took an Assistant Pastorship in a rapidly growing rural church. Mom worked at Wright-Patterson Air Force Base some twenty miles from home. I was left in the care of my mother's mother. Her name was Viola Bowser. She had given her husband Carl two daughters, Mary Ruth and Marda Marie. We lived in a prefabricated home behind the Bowser residence. It was small but adequate for our needs. In the mornings, I'd go to Grandma's house for a breakfast of oatmeal, toast and a glass of orange juice. I would then walk to Rockway Elementary School about a mile from home.

School was living hell for me in those early days up north. The other kids made fun of my deep southern accent. I was called hick, rebel or hillbilly. My spelling reflected my deep accent. Instead of writing the word right, I would write "rat." Got the picture? I spelled things phonetically! Southern schools were not as advanced and the possibility of putting me back to the second grade horrified me. I struggled to keep up. I was not going to let these damned Yankees get the best of me! Ironic, was it not?

My advancement in school seemed to be going on at a snails pace. I was the smallest boy in the class year after year. Needless to say, I became the butt of many jokes. I learned to fight as best

I could. There was this kid who had failed the fifth grade and he took it out on me! His name was Bob. Compared to me, he was a giant! He played first-string full back in junior high school. I was second-string right guard. There was one thing that I could do better than any body else in those days. I had learned to out-run everybody! The school coach put me on first string 100 and 200-yard dashes, and 400-yard relay! I gathered points for Rockway Junior High! We didn't win the championship, but we weren't at the bottom either. Mr. Hackle said, "John, if it had been other than combined point scoring, you would have won it for us." That made me feel very superior! Problem was, I heard that word before from someone else in a completely different and much darker setting.

My adoptive mother's father had worked for years at the International Harvester Truck factory. He was a skilled tool and dye man. He was also a flaming alcoholic. He had this thing about going out on binges for days on end. One time he returned with boxes of clothing that he couldn't remember buying! Another incident was the bringing home of three baby goats and a lamb. No one knows where they came from, he simply could not remember! He had an even darker side that came out when he stayed at home and drank in his basement.

His family ancestry was German. He had been a member of the German-American Bund before World War Two. He and his brothers idolized a man with a funny little mustache in their Fatherland – Adolph Hitler. Carl – I will not call him Grandfather for reasons, which shall become apparent – held on to his "unshakable belief" in the superiority of the Aryan Races. He would call me into the garage and talk about the good old days when Nazism came close to ruling the world. He began to give me shots of whiskey as a reward for listening. I was twelve years old at that time.

He introduced me to Nazi and Nordic mythology that focused on the nude human form. Eventually, he convinced me that if I wished to be acceptable by him and his friends, I needed to be "initiated." More of the same abuse as years before came my way. I began to sniff glue and gasoline to kill the shame and physical pain I felt within. One of the main issues that any "survivor of abuse" must face is why they dare not tell anyone what was going on! When you're twelve years old and you are told that no one will believe you, it makes sense. How could I tell my mother what her father was doing? The family laughed off whatever antic he pulled. He was a very skillful manipulator. So, I endured the shame and physical pain alone rationalizing it all away. I told myself that if that is what it took to be a good Nazi, then so be it! I'd whip up the fascist salute for Carl and shout, "Zeig Hiel!" I read volumes of books on the glory of the Third Reich. I began to have this sense of power when I discussed what should be done to Papists, Jews, and yes, Negroes. Grotesque pictures of emaciated bodies in pits became my daily mental diet. Hate seemed so wonderful; it killed the pain; and, I didn't have to look at myself! I could blame everything on others. How convenient! I buried the only love I had ever known in a venom-laced coffin of empty rhetoric. "Dark forces" that I heard about in church, but did not take seriously, had set me up. Time and again, they would enter my warped life style.

Nazism was in the news in 1959. Israeli agents had captured Adolph Eichman who helped master mind the Final Solution, other wise know as the Holocaust. He was on trial for "crimes against humanity?" My rationale was this: How can that be when Jews and others are non-human vermin to be wiped out? I eagerly watched the news each evening for information on a real Nazi hero. The kids at school shunned me. I didn't care! There was this awesome narcotic ruling my mind called race hate. I was finally "somebody," or so I thought!

My opinions on political matters were decidedly far to the right. Communism had to be eradicated by any means necessary. Lord knows Hitler tried and failed! Now it was America's duty to stand in the gap for "white freedom." My parents became very concerned. Teachers and the Principal at Rockway had discussed my antics. Finally, I found myself sitting at the desk of a kindly gentleman who listened to me rant and rave about how Jews needed to be gassed! He never contradicted my views – not once. I thought I had gained a new convert for George Lincoln Rockwell, Presidential Candidate of the American Nazi Party - just like he said to do! Our session was over. The Counselor quietly said he'd like to see me in a week, if I was agreeable to that. I shook his hand and left his office.

The next week came and I found myself across from this kind and seemingly understanding gentleman. He asked me how I had been doing. My reply was matter-of-fact, "Okay in spite of the lies about Colonel Eichman." He leaned back in his chair and studied my face very carefully. Finally, he asked a point-blank question that rocked my little poison-laden boat. He said, "John, have you ever met a Jew before?" I could feel my face become a frowning mass. "Hell no! And, I don't want to! You can't trust those pawn brokers." I sat silently waiting for some sort of response. He flipped the subject by asking me what I thought of him. I said that he seemed like a very nice man who genuinely cared about me. He said, "We only met last week. Are you sure you think I'm a nice man that cares about you?" My face reflected puzzlement as I said, "I can tell you're a very nice person!" He said, "Thank you, John. That means a lot to me." I shrugged my shoulders. There was a long pause as he studied my face more intently. He then said, "John, what would you think if I said I am a Jew?" I sat stunned and began to rise out of the chair. He motioned for me to sit back down. He slowly leaned forward and said, "My parents died in a place called Majdanek which is the death camp next to Aulschwitz. A Roman Catholic family near Munich hid me until after the war. John, before you decide to hate me, wouldn't it be a good idea to get to know me first?" He sat back in his chair and observed my reaction to his words. I said nothing. I felt my face going blank. He smiled and said, "John, before you decide anything else, I would be honored to take you to my synagogue next Friday. There will be lots of good food and fun." I politely declined his invitation, but I never forgot his kindness in spite of my venom. I remained a political conservative for years after, but never again did I give a fascist salute. I began to see Carl for what he was, a very sick human being who probably had done to him what he had done to me. Years later in 1992, I told my Mother what had happened after grueling therapy that I sorely needed. She began to cry on the telephone because she too had been a victim. We haven't spoken since. Why? In her mind, she doesn't need therapy. As a retired Counselor today, I agree. At her age, it would probably kill her to relive all the shame and pain that she endured so many years ago. She's in my prayers where she belongs and nothing more. *If you really love someone, you let him, or her, choose his or her own destiny even if it hurts him or her. Everyone must learn their own lessons in their own way. The only thing we can do is to provide good information, a nonjudgmental attitude, be there if they come around and pray for them. Only God Almighty has control, not us!*

High school was pretty much a breeze. I had a few dates and went to a dance or two, but deep inside I longed for something. I was running on empty! I didn't have a clue! I got a job in the deli department of a large grocery store. I enjoyed working because it paid for my 1955 white on green Chevy four-door sedan. I had become the envy of most of the other guys in school because I did have my own wheels. I had somehow latched on to a hard work ethic and became a compulsive saver. My senior year was a blast. My best friend Jim and I sped around in my wheels attempting to impress girls.

I hit my eighteenth birthday and decided not to have a party. What I did instead began a downward spiral that lasted until age forty-three! The behavior was that of a diseased person. I drove all the way across town to a liquor store. I purchased a couple of six packs of what was known as 3.2 beer in those days. I then drove several miles out of town to a park. I sat alone and began to drink the gnawing pain of my past away. Only a real alcoholic can identify with the sense of relief and ease it gave me. I had a liquid lover, a friend and confidant for life! Although I dabbled in whiskey with Carl and sniffed glue and gasoline at age 12, this stuff was "legal"; seemingly far less harmful; and, I wanted more. Just before my graduation, the Ohio State Police stopped me for speeding. Fortunately, I had no beer cans in the car at the time. I went to jail and waited for my stepfather to come get their wayward brat out! My adoptive father had passed in 1962.

I graduated somewhere in the middle of my class standing. I had a flare for history, especially World War Two. In June of 1965, I entered the U.S. Air Force basic training facility near San

Antonio, Texas – Lackland A.F.B. Another chapter of my life was beginning that would lead me half way around the world and back again with truly tragic results. I would never be the same! ***Our perception of reality is rarely what it actually is. Awareness of our environment and our selves is paramount to our survival!***

Chapter Three
Uniforms

The Boeing 707 seemed to shoot up into the air like a rocket and banked hard to the left. We were headed southwest towards what I honestly believed was the land of buffaloes, cowboys, steers, Indians and oil wells. The plane touched down some three hours later. Eight of us had joined the Air Force together from Springfield, Ohio. Our picture was in the paper! We prided ourselves in being so important, or so we thought as we milled around the San Antonio Airport. A stalky Hispanic fellow in highly starched fatigues walked up to us in the lobby and very kindly escorted us to a waiting blue bus. Once the doors were closed, he began to spit fire. He called us "girls!" The guy sitting next to me near the rear made the mistake of saying, "Oh shit!" The Drill Instructor ran back and started screaming, "Which one of you bitches said that?" I looked out the window and played dumb in a hurry. I thought to myself: "Oh my God, what have I done?"

We reached the basic training facility about forty-five minutes later. The bus lurched to a stop in front of a large wooden building complex known as the "Green Monster." We filed out into the darkness to await further orders from Speedy Gonzales as some were starting to call him. Sure enough, he started yelling again as we moved forward. We lined up at a counter where Government

Issue pillow, case, sheets, and one very coarse blanket became our temporary property. We filed back onto the bus and rode for what seemed an eternity. The time was about 0300 hours when we arrived at our new home – a barracks! We slept four to a room. I chose a top bunk because I did not want anyone falling on top of me in the middle of the night!

The next morning we were awakened at 0700 hours. We leisurely walked to the Mess Hall where we received "SOS." Please do not ask me to translate the letters. I will let you figure it out! We gulped down chipped beef in white gravy on a slice of toast with a side glass of orange juice. We went back to the barracks in slow fashion and waited for what seemed hours. Suddenly, out of nowhere two highly starched fatigue-wearing men arrived in the barracks. I began to think we were in Mexico! Both men had the same name – Gonzales. They seemed to be waiting for some fool to say, "Speedy." We were rushed outside and told to line up. Have you ever heard of a Chinese Fire Drill? I am sure we must have looked ridiculous to other troops passing by. After all, we still had our hair and could not even line up correctly!

The next few days went by very rapidly. Our heads were shaven. Our civilian clothing was bundled up and we began to look and sound much the same. Military orders were hammered into our pea brains. We received shots, lessons on polishing boots, how to march in time, don't sit on the hot pavement cause it will give you hemorrhoids, don't look toward the women – WAFS - marching by, write your mother a letter, kiss your butt good bye, and don't forget to salute the officers. Whew! We all filled out what was called a Dream Sheet. It was a request for whatever job you may wish to pursue and were qualified for, if it were available. I chose Chaplainry Corps, Medical Corps or Air Police. Our Drill Instructor told all of us to put in for Air Police Training because that is what he was at one time. Our training continued for ten more weeks and then came the orders for duty stations. I was headed for Gunter A.F.B. near Montgomery, Alabama for Medical Corps training! Little did I realize what I had gotten myself into.

The troop train pulled into Old Union Station in downtown Houston, Texas in the beginning of August, 1965. We waited for what seemed a lifetime for civilians to board the train headed eastward. I remember saying to myself, "God damn it, I will never step foot in the State of Texas again!" Those words would come back to haunt me years later as I re-entered Houston in 1970. The old train station became an apartment building for U.S. Veterans. It is the very location where this book was written! God does have a sense of humor!

The heat and humidity of Alabama in the summer time is sweltering. At least San Antonio had low humidity. Jim, one of the original eight from Springfield, had received the same orders as I. We decided to room together with a fellow by the name of Sam. He was black! Really black! I've only seen maybe three other African Americans as dark has him. He was a likable cuss from South Carolina. We seemed to gel very well together. We all liked the same music that ranged from rock to rhythm and blues. We attended classes together and hung out at the Airmen's Club TOGETHER!

We watched the news one evening as a place called Watts in Los Angeles went up in flames. Jim and I both observed Sam begin to shed a tear. He walked off and said nothing the rest of the night. Later in the month, we heard of problems brewing in Montgomery. It seemed that airmen were being attacked while on pass. They were supposed to be guilty of "mixing." Gender was not necessarily the issue, any airmen together of different races had become fair game. Keeping in mind that the March from Selma had taken place some five months earlier, nerves were raw. Bobby Kennedy had begun to force the issue of integration big time. The federal government was looking for ways to leverage power over the segregationists. Sure enough, the "States Rights" good old boys gave them a reason and just what the Feds were looking for.

Our entire barracks was called in for a special meeting on a Friday morning. A Major walked into the hall as we snapped to attention. We sat down and he began to divulge information about racial incidents involving airmen on pass and Klan member activity. He said that he was not ordering the base to be shut down as had been rumored. He would allow any airman the freedom to transverse as they so chose in the streets of Montgomery. He then said that those airmen venturing off base on pass would be considered "volunteers." He said he couldn't make us go on pass, but those who did might get a Letter of Commendation. He said that it could be dangerous and walked out of the room as we snapped to attention again. The room became a buzz of questions.

Jim, Sam and I made our way back to our room. No one said a word for over an hour; and, no one turned on the radio. We just sat on our bunks silently. Finally, Jim said, "I wonder what's playing at the theater downtown tomorrow?" Sam grunted something to the effect, "Beats me." I said, "So when's the bus leave for town tomorrow morning?" That question brought back the silence. Sam looked at Jim and then at me and said, "Are you thinking what I think you're thinking?" Jim and I both nodded in the affirmative. Sam said, "Why?" I raised my thumbs up and proudly said, "Air Force!" Sam's eyes became perfectly circular showing white all around his irises. We all said, "Right on!" at the same time.

It was Labor Day Weekend when we took the city shuttle downtown. Our destination was near the foot of the State Capital Building. We had a camera with us and looked pretty much like uniformed tourists. The three of us sauntered our way up the incline to the capital steps. Jim shrugged his shoulders and we began the climb. We reached the top of the steps and noticed what looked like a Mogan David, Star of David, near a Romanesque pillar. I read the inscription that simply stated: "On this spot Jefferson Davis was sworn in as the first President of the Confederate States of America." Jim and I smiled at each other and Sam seemed horrified. I said, "Come on Sam." I took his hand and we shook over the star. Jim took the shot. I said, "Air Force, all the way!" We walked down the steps and toward a nearby theater where we watched "North to Alaska" starring John Wayne.

We decided to return to the base around four that hot afternoon. We walked to an unfamiliar bus stop and wondered which line to take back. There was a black lady waiting patiently for her arrival. I walked over to ask which bus line went back to Gunter. She had a puzzled look on her face and hesitated for a moment She then told me the correct line. I thanked her and turned to tell the others that I had obtained the information we needed. They had wandered off to a nearby store window when suddenly I felt a sharp object over my right kidney. A male voice with a deep southern drawl and very bad tobacco breath said, "You don't talk to niggers down here! Get your damn Yankee ass back where you came from." The lady had disappeared! Jim turned toward me and looked at my face. He said, "What's wrong, John?" I didn't say anything. I just pointed to my back. Sam came over and looked. He said, "Damn man, you're bleeding!" I said angrily, "No shit! And, where the hell were you two? What happened to the black lady?" I must have looked at them as if they were from another planet. There I stood bleeding, which ruined a perfectly good summer Class A uniform shirt. I was angry because I felt let down by my own. This wasn't about race relations for me. It was an issue of military pride, nothing more. I must be honest about that at this point!

We arrived back on base. We reported to the Officer of the Day who took our deposition. I was treated and released with a minor stab wound to the back. I did receive a Letter of Commendation. Our Flight was one of the last to go through Gunter. It was closed deliberately by the federal government in retaliation for several actions against military personnel. All medical training to this day is in Shepherd A.F.B. in northern Texas. God only knows how many millions of dollars in income was lost to Montgomery because of a few willfully ignorant men in sheets.

The last week of training was approaching for our Flight. A flight is the equivalent of a platoon in the Army. We gathered in a hanger suited up in battle gear complete with all appropriate survival utensils. Our group of happy campers was mixed – meaning genders. We all had gone through training on how to give shots, extract blood, various bandages, tourniquets, splints, and rules of war for escorting wounded off the battlefield. Now, it was time to find out if we had learned anything. We were headed to the swamps! We were marched some ten miles out to an area covered with mud, cypress knuckles, more mud, a small stream about ten feet wide, and of course more mud. We went through drills on getting a wounded GI over the stream with only two ten-foot poles.

We had to lift wounded GIs on stretchers over a ten-foot wall in full gear with smoke bombs going off all around us.

Our final evening was truly a nightmare. We were marched out into what really was a swamp complete with Spanish moss hanging from tree limbs, greenish-black pools of water and snakes! We were teamed up in couples. Each tandem was given a small flashlight, a compass, and coordinates to follow. Our objective was to get back to camp in the least amount of time as possible. There was only one African American female in the Flight. The leader called her name. He then called mine, much to my chagrin! We were blindfolded and led to our jumping off point. From then on, we were on our own! We had all night to get back, if we didn't get lost first. Then we would face graduation the next day!

I've heard it said that if you really want to get to know someone, go on a camping trip together. Whoever said that is absolutely correct. This "WAF" was a country girl from Alabama and knew her stuff about swamps. She held the light and I figured coordinates. She had a problem with numbers. But when it came to telling distances, she was a natural. Furlongs and that sort of thing are what she grew up with! We arrived back in camp and waited for the timed results of each team. She and I won to the amazement of most, and the snickers of others. We marched back to the main base "together." We were tired, hungry and stunk to high heaven. That green slime floating in the water had stuck to us!

The next night our Flight got together for a farewell party at the Airmen's Club. The Flight Commander congratulated the gathering and gave out certificates signifying our successful completion. There was a dance after the commencement. I went over and asked that farm girl to dance. We hit the floor and began to boogie. After all, we were a team, and the best at that! I would not have admitted it publicly, but I was very proud of her. The next day it was time to go our separate ways. I went home on leave for a few days and then on to my first permanent duty station – Fairchild A.F.B. near Spokane, Washington. My life was to take a radical turn in the next three years. ***God gives us what we need when we need it - even black angels!***

Chapter Four
Shades of Abuse

My first two and a half years at Spokane, Washington were tumultuous. I had entered a relationship with a Japanese-Filipino girl from Hawaii. She attended a nearby Catholic Women's College. We dated often, but the basis for a lasting union was not there. I was a Protestant and she would not marry out of her faith! She was most adamant on that subject. Finally, we went our separate ways although we continued to correspond after I was transferred to my next duty station at Westover A.F.B. near Springfield, Massachusetts.

At first, I longed to be back in the Great Northwest. I missed the clear, crisp air and the distant western foothills of the Rocky Mountains. There was plenty to do. Water skiing in the summer and snowball fights in the winter. I missed the "cherry" 1957 classic Chevy coup I had purchased. It had gold trim. What a beautiful machine; and what a beautiful part of God's world. My heart was troubled and I began to drink more heavily. I began to experience what are known as "black outs." I appeared perfectly normal except I couldn't remember what I had done the night before! Sounds just like Carl, doesn't it?

Another issue kept coming up. When I was stationed near Spokane, I received a call from a person who said she was my mother! I was curious because my Mother and I had not communicated in quite some time. The voice on the other end of the line introduced herself as Mabel Stevens. She did her best to respect my wishes, which were that I already had a mother, and please don't call me again! About two months later, I was called into the Commander's office. He informed me that my mother had died. I was in shock! I called the number I knew and my Mother answered the telephone. She informed me that indeed my birth mother had passed away. She was only thirty-six years old at her death!

The flight back to Springfield, Ohio went without a hitch. I was on Emergency Leave. My Aunt Irene picked me up at the airport near Dayton. We rode to her home as Irene related to me about her sister Mabel. That evening, we went over to the funeral home where I had a talk with the Director. He gave me the sad details of Mabel's last days. She suffered from horrible bouts of depression. She had become an alcoholic and drug addict. She made her living in bars "selling love." It seems that she could no longer handle what she was doing and longed for the one thing she had lost in her teenage years – her baby boy. I sat there stunned. I could feel myself becoming numb. I said nothing.

Irene and I walked over to her casket and viewed her motionless face. Although deceased, she was a very attractive woman. She had jet-black very wavy hair and light brown, or very tanned, complexion. What I was looking at was my true roots, but I didn't know it at that time what Black-Irish meant. No one in the family ever mentioned the African connection! That evening began with my experiencing deep guilt within while playing the "If Only Game." Years later, a kind therapist explained that Mabel had made her own choices, which came back to haunt her. I was not responsible for her demise. *Make sure the baggage you're carrying is only yours. Others will attempt to load theirs upon you, if you permit it.*

My state of mind at Westover continued to deteriorate. Then suddenly, a new member entered the Medical Team at the dental clinic where I worked. Patty was an absolute knock out! She stood five feet four inches tall and had a perfect figure. Every man around asked her out, but usually to no avail. She was choosy and could afford to be. We began working together in the oral hygiene area. I trained her in cleaning techniques. She had sparkling, deep brown eyes; black wavy hair; and, a tan complexion. She was white but with a twist. Her mother was Scandinavian and her father was Jewish. She hailed from Southern California. I had been there a few times in my travels so we had that in common. She also liked my VW Bug because she had owned one before entering the Air Force. Two things in common! She was a church going girl although Protestant. I attended Mass and had been baptized Roman Catholic to please the Hawaiian Princess! I began attending church with the California Dreamer on a regular basis. We began dating much to the chagrin of other males. Eventually, we became engaged. Things were going great and then stuff hit the fan!

Orders came down for my transfer to Korea. Communist North Korea had captured an intelligence ship known as the U.S.S. Pueblo. Kansas and Ohio State National Guard Units were hastily called up for active duty. They held down the fort, so to speak, until regular troops could arrive. I was one of those. I said my good byes to my fiancée whom I would never see again. I did not know that at the time!

Korea was like nothing I had ever seen before. It was hot that August day when the troop plane touched down at Kimpo Field near Seoul. U.S. dollars were exchanged for what was called MPCs, or Military Payment Certificates. It looked very much like play money having different colors. I boarded a bus southward to Osan Air Base. There I awaited further orders that came rapidly. I was headed for K-8 otherwise known as Kunsan Air Base. The word "kun" means gold in the Korean language. Pure gold was for sale for pennies on the dollar, if you had dollars! That's why GIs carried the script instead to discourage black market trade in gold.

My new barracks home had been built by Japanese Imperial Air Force personnel way back in 1938! The corrugated steel top resounded with every drop of rain that fell. Flies seemed to be everywhere and the stench of human and animal waste from nearby rice paddies was sickening. Beer was actually prescribed through the dispensary where I worked to encourage guys to eat!

I spent my first few days on base being oriented. In the evenings, I hit the Noncommissioned Officer's Club. I had made Sergeant by then. I drank like a fish. I also tried my hand at the one-armed bandits (slot machines). I usually won by waiting until they were full!

My Specialty Code was 98150, or Dental Assistant. The doctor I worked with was fairly young and a devout Catholic. We took trips together around the countryside with the other dental assistant who was a very attractive Korean female. The doctor and I loved to play tricks on patients who expressed reluctance to come in for treatments. I'd make what looked like firecrackers out of cotton roles dipped in iodine with dental floss as a make-believe fuse. The doctor would place it in the patient's mouth and pretend to light the fuse. We stood back with our fingers in our ears waiting for the blast! Truth is, we acted the part of ugly Americans!

Eventually, I was allowed off base. I ended up helping Military Public Health personnel round up the local "business girls"- as they called themselves - for blood tests. My first job in Korea was testing girls for venereal diseases. That's where I met "Linda" who was a very attractive twenty-five year old that knew her "profession." She took a liking to me because I appeared so young. She'd call me "baby face." She decided that I would be her "dream lover." This is where we take a break from the story to examine the world of prostitution up close and personal. Regardless of time period, ethnicity or location, the scenario is pretty much the same everywhere!

Most prostitutes are "broken in" usually by a male relative through sexual abuse. Her ego is smashed and then she is ready to do the bidding of her "protector" – the pimp. He makes sure she stays out of jail and from beatings from "johns." These are her customers she usually calls "dates." In exchange for his services, the pimp receives everything the prostitute makes. He clothes her for work. He transports her to clients. He controls every aspect of her life. She performs and delivers. How well she performs is reflected in how prosperous the pimp is. There is a dark side. The pimp will beat her within an inch of her life if she so much as thinks about leaving the lifestyle. In the case of older prostitutes, they are simply killed off or abandoned by their pimps to fend for themselves. No beauty, no "johns" except for what she may drum up in seedy bars.

The prostitute's life is a precarious one at best! It is dangerous either in clubs, or on the streets. Violence occurs regularly and the specter of disease gnaws at the psyche. Good reason for her to find some sort of mental coping skill to perform her daily tasks. Enter the "dream lover." He is the object of her affection. She may see him infrequently, but when they are together, she enters a fantasy world of the faithful wife and lover. He gets "freebies." When she is not with him, she fantasizes about him while performing sexual acts with "johns." That's the only way she can continue to do what she does without losing her mind completely. Problem is, another personality is formed in due time to associate with the "dream lover" and still another for the "johns." She continues her downward spiral into Disassociative Personality Disorder also known as Multiple Personality Complex. In her fantasy world she can enjoy sexual release because her "lover" is with her at all times. I learned of this when doing research for a Psychology paper in college. I spent considerable time with the Houston Police Vice Squad to obtain information on deviant sex - in 1992. In Korea (1968); I got to know a number of girls very well. They loved to talk because someone is actually giving them what they crave – attention! Most begin to cry eventually because like my own birth mother, they have kids somewhere. It's pretty much the same the world over. My heart goes out to them because their lives really are a living hell behind the façade of smiles and make up. It is said that Jesus had a special place in His large heart for Mary Magdalene. Perhaps we may understand more clearly just, how gentle, loving and kind He really is! ***Take care not to judge others, least you be judged! No one is guilt free!***

Time slipped by rapidly and the season was becoming decidedly colder. The California Dreamer and I had split up. I got drunk one night and wrote her parents a letter filled with anger and cursing. They sent the letter to her and the relationship was off. I seemed not to care anymore about anything. I just wanted to get drunk and "use" Linda. She would give me food, clothing, sex and then bed me in before she went to "work." She had girl friends that were looking for someone to dream about, especially the new girls. Linda was very enterprising. She shared me with girls she broke in so they could do their thing. She acquired a couple of taxicabs and had drivers working around the clock. She knew the life style she had would not last forever, so she was preparing for when she began to wrinkle and sag. I lived like a king! Linda had "baby face" and as long as I didn't get too involved with her other girls, she was willing to share.

One of her girls introduced me to a drink called Portoju. It was a sweet wine laced with opium. I loved it! Eventually, I was hooked. Linda found out and put out a contract of death on the girl. Linda literally nursed me back to some semblance of sanity. She fed me, bathed me and sang Korean lullabies to me. I showed my gratitude by becoming distant. Down deep inside I knew what I was doing was dead wrong. She checked on me constantly. Eventually, I returned to her clutches only to despise her for "using" me. What a hypocrite I was!

In the mean time, the Hawaiian Princess wrote me a letter! We began corresponding regularly. I agreed to become a Confirmed Catholic. The Bishop for that region of Korea performed the Mass with my dentist friend as my "sponsor." The Hawaiian Princess was overjoyed, and we agreed to meet in Hawaii over Easter of 1969. The trip was arduous, but worth it. We spent two weeks in the sun, surf and sand. I presented her with an engagement ring. She was a happy camper at last. I was happy also, for the time being. My return to Korea would change all that!

I shall not go into details as to what happened next, but to say that I became involved in netharious goings on is putting it mildly. My lifestyle became dark indeed! Smuggling became a part of routine daily fair. People disappeared. I was back on opium again! Linda was furious. My Commander called me in and wondered what was going on in my career. I lied through my eyeteeth! My hands began to shake. I couldn't eat. I was losing control of my senses. Eventually, I fell apart and voluntarily went in for drug rehabilitation at Tachikawa A.F.B. near Tokyo, Japan. I was shipped back to Wright-Patterson A.F.B. to remain in a psyche ward for the next six months. God was looking out for me because I obtained an Honorable Discharge in spite of my foolishness. Instead of being grateful, I was bitter and crushed! ***God's mercy is unlimited! Why is it that we cannot give ourselves what God gives so freely? Forgiveness!***

Chapter Five
Disillusionment

Civilian life was something I had to get used to all over again. I felt lost without orders from "higher ups." I had to think for myself, and make choices! My mind-set was one of dependence upon a Big Brother to see me through. My head was full of memories of Lackland, Gunter, Fairchild, Westover and then Kunsan. Names and faces raced through my head as I listened to my seven-inch reel-to-reel tape recorder complete with Pioneer speakers I had purchased overseas. There was a crate in my parent's garage from Massachusetts. I knew whom it was from – California Girl. She had sent everything back to me in care of my parents! One more heart wrenching memory!

Eventually, I landed an excellent position at Toro Manufacturing, Inc. assembling power-riding mowers for the dwellers of our nation's suburbs. I was paid union wages and bought a new car. It was a Cortez silver 1970 Chevy Nova with black interior. I put an eight-track tape deck in it. My first tape was of the "Jackson 5!" When I wasn't out cruising, I attended college at night studying basic drawing. I met an elementary school teacher gathering extra credits for a new teaching position. We hit it off from the get go. Within a week, we were living a life of debauchery and getting drunk almost every night. I felt empty and alone – living inside my head filled with painful memories of days gone by was like being a member of the "walking dead."

News came from Kent State University that was horrendous. Students were shot for demonstrating against the Viet Nam War. That brought back memories of demonstrations within the military against the same war of which I had been an undercover informant for military intelligence against the "peaceniks." I had been a die hard Goldwater-Nixon Republican and proud of it! My mind wandered back to 1968.

I recalled when Rev. Doctor Martin Luther King, Jr. was assassinated. A fellow named Bob and I located our selves in the streets surveying what was going on near Westover. There had been threats to bomb the base. We acted as a couple of drunks bar hopping while searching for information. No one knew what we were doing off base, not even California Girl! In a way, my personality had already begun to split like the whores I later lived with in Korea. My "dream lover" was power brought on by a false sense of self-importance. I craved that egomaniacal feeling that masked the insecurity that was gnawing away at me constantly. Alcohol helped to lubricate my journey into an emotional fantasyland.

A Sunday school teacher from the church I attended before going into the service gave me a call one evening of spring, 1970. He invited me to come visit his class some weekend. At first, I was reluctant, but being true to the "people pleaser" I had become, I just couldn't flat out say, "No." I kept my word and went back to church where one fateful Sunday morning, I actually went down to the altar for prayer. The teacher came over and we went to another room. I told him the gut level truth that I didn't trust anybody anymore, not even God. He never condemned me. He told me that my generation had a lot not to trust! Young men were coming home in body bags, strung out on heroine, Hepatitis B and C as part of biological warfare, cancers from Agent Orange, and branded as "baby killers" by the general population! I just sat there and began to weep as the teacher looked on. I started shouting, "God damn it!" over and over again. He was crying also. His son had just joined the Navy. This was in June of 1970. Little did I realize I would soon begin a trip of no return from Springfield, Ohio! There was no welcome home for us veterans! Home wasn't there anymore, if it ever was. My age of innocence had been smashed all to hell forever! ***The consequences of our behavior are much like dropping a pebble in a quiet pond. Ripples go out and return to us eventually.***

Chapter Six
Religion and Rebellion

In early August , 1970, I received notice that I had been accepted at Gulf Coast Bible College in Houston, Texas. I said farewell to my Mother and her husband Alex. I drove to the Sunday school teacher's home for a quick prayer and I was on the road again. The trip was uneventful until I entered Mississippi. My Ohio State license plates stuck out like a proverbial sore thumb. I stopped in mid state near Jackson because I was "dog tired." The next morning as I left the motor lodge, the local police followed me for several miles. My mind went back to Montgomery in 1965. I had good reason to stay within the speed limit and watch my rear view mirror. Finally, the Louisiana State line made me glad to be out of Mississippi.

I hit the outskirts of Houston, Texas about 8:00PM Central Time. I had no idea how large Houston had become since 1965! I can still remember zooming down I-10 West and seeing a large rotating Gulf Oil sign on top of a skyscraper. I got off at Heights Boulevard and turned left on West 11th Street. The school lay just ahead. The Historic Heights would become my home for the next twenty years! I lost my fortune more than once, but somehow bounced back in The Heights. God was with me in spite of *me*!

My first school year was mostly uneventful. I attended classes and stayed to my self. I worked a night security job and attended classes in the mornings. Much to my surprise, I made the Dean's List the second semester! The routine was boring for me. I longed for some sort of action, excitement, or more to the point – mischief. Although I professed a saving knowledge in Jesus, I secretly hated all the conservative rules and regulations. I drove off campus and began to drink again. Oh what a feeling! My troubles were washed away with a few gulps of ice-cold draft. I drank on the job as well. A client in the building supplied me with shots of whiskey to "keep me alert." I met a cute little Hispanic chick that was more than willing to fall into my arms. Later on, I learned that she was going through the process of divorce from a domestic violence type. My interest soon waned and I moved on to the next emotional hostage I could find. Down deep inside, I felt like garbage. It seemed I couldn't help myself.

I went the summer semester to speed up the process of getting out of GBC. I applied at a west coast university and was accepted. Problem was, I would have lost a year of credits. So, I decided to remain in Houston. I quit the security job and went to work in a supply warehouse filling orders for semi truck delivery all over eastern Texas. The pay was good and the bosses took a liking to me.

My second year became more tumultuous. A lady who lived near the school and attended the campus church befriended me. We'd have coffee together and I played with her two kids. I knew she was married, but her husband was never around. It seems that he was a workaholic. She desired companionship and I kindly obliged. We began going out for dinners together. Eventually, she came on to me one evening. I must admit she looked good, but I had enough sense to realize her proximity to the school and associations there would mean disaster. I very politely declined and withdrew within myself again. My forays to gulp beer didn't stop.

Something inside of me began to bubble to the surface. There was this deep anger that began to consume me. I had no idea what it meant! I became very depressed and entertained the idea of suicide. I used whatever I could get my hands on to get to sleep at night. I felt as though my life was going down a giant toilet. My

roommate from Oklahoma sensed my anguish and told the new
Dean of Students. He was a Psychologist as well as Professor.
He referred me to the local Veteran's Administration Hospital. I
was put on anti-depressant medication for a time. I seemed to be
pulling out of the slump. My grades began to rise again, thank
God!

Toward the end of my second year, students urged me to run
for Editor of the school paper. I began a campaign based on liberal
reforms. I promised new sections on arts and crafts, guaranteed
freedom of speech for faculty as well as students, ending the local
gossip column, stressing academics over religiosity and a cartoon
each week. I was elected by a landslide vote! A feverish pitch of
excitement ran through the school as students lined up to be a part
of something really worthwhile. The entire format was changed,
and I kept my word with the first edition. I received a roaring
applause in chapel about the new paper. It seemed that I was on a
roll.

A Dorm Mother for the ladies building approached me with
a problem. She related how one of her "kids" was having trouble
fitting in. She asked if I could speak with the girl and cheer her
up. I agreed. She informed me that the girl had a history of drug
abuse. She knew that I had done drugs before. However, she did
not know about my drinking. She brought the girl to me for a talk.
She was strikingly attractive with big brown eyes, long pale blonde
hair and had a thing for wearing black all the time.

We began seeing each other on a purely platonic basis. I took
her on a pick nick in a field of flowers near Houston. We lay on
a blanket and nature began to work its magic. Yes, magic! She
began incantations. As the day wore on, she revealed that she
was indeed a witch sent to GBC against her will by her concerned
parents. She had always worn long sleeved black blouses. She
rolled up her sleeves and showed me her track marks. She
informed me that she loved meth amphetamine - "speed", it helped
her get in touch with the "spirit world" quicker! Then she put
her arms around my neck and pulled me down upon her. Need I
say more? We became somewhat of an item. The paper that had
begun so well began to slip in quality. The staff wondered where I

was at meetings. Someone said that the girl was going off campus to cavort in the night. She was brought into the Dean's Office and told that she would have to leave at the end of the semester. I lay low, but agreed to take her back to her home in Missouri over Christmas break.

I dropped her off and headed back to Ohio to see family. It was short lived. It just wasn't the same. I felt out of place and left early in a new 1973 Oldsmobile Omega I purchased at a local dealership. Meanwhile back in Missouri, the girl had planned a party in my honor. She had her girl friends come over to her "dealer's" house. I was the only male as I sat in a circle with thirteen females. A large bong (a from of water pipe) was passed from person to person until a half-ounce chip of Lebanese blonde hashish was consumed through a quart of Everclear (pure alcohol)! We drank Vodka Collins laced with Orange Sunshine (LSD). The party was on. Needless to say, I was back to my old lifestyle I thought I had left in Korea, this time with worse results. ***What goes around keeps coming around until we choose to change what we are doing.***

My return to school was uneventful. Everything seemed to be routine except for this gnawing unease in the pit of my stomach. My nights became sleepless, and my days were filled with high anxiety. Concentration on studies became increasingly difficult. Work became meaningless. I stopped caring about the school newspaper. My life seemed to be on the edge of an abyss of despair and despondency. I was being consumed by something beyond my control. I was moving head long toward disaster!

The Dean of Students referred me back to the VA Hospital. I stood in their Psychiatric Center dripping blood on the floor. Both wrists had been cut. The bandages placed on my arms by the school nurse were soaked to over flowing. My life was a shambles. The doctor at the VA didn't seem to care. No one seemed to understand, not even God! I had hit a new all time low in my life. Somehow, in this process I began to piece together the concept that my behaviors had consequences! I returned to my school dorm room and knelt down. Tears began to flow as I hugged a Bible. Something inside of me began to let go. Suddenly, what mattered didn't. I rose to my feet several minutes later with what seemed like an answer. ***There's one thing I've learned in life – when I think I know something for sure, I probably don't! Total dependence upon a loving God is an absolute necessity!***

The end of my third year at GBC was coming to a close. I was asked to step down from my position as Editor of the school newspaper. Other students shunned me. I was ready to move on to whatever might come my way. My job at the warehouse was saved in spite of the suicide attempt. I kept the new car and moved into a small garage apartment in the Houston Heights. Life seemed less complicated. I began building an N-scale model railroad in my small bedroom. That helped to while away off time from work. My life had become simplified, and I had a modicum of peace, or so I thought.

The model railroad became a passion. It helped heal a hurt from my adolescent days. Just before Christmas in my eleventh year of existence, I observed a Marx Model Railroad set in a department store window in downtown Springfield. It was only $19.95! I tugged on my Mother's coat sleeve and said, "That's what I would really like to have for Christmas. Can I have it please?" She carefully looked at it through the glass and replied, "I think it's time you learned that money doesn't grow on trees. If you want something like that, work for it!" I was crushed. It was only a small amount of cost. How could I raise money to buy this train? Then it occurred to me that by the time, I raised the money, the train might be gone! I became more disheartened. It seemed I couldn't win in life. I was given a very small weekly allowance. I opened up a school savings account and determined to save what I needed to get that train. I raked leaves, mowed yards and delivered newspapers. It took almost six months, but I did get a train set – bigger and better than the one in the window. I kept it until I left for Texas in 1970! ***The harder a person has to work for any goal, the more valuable that goal is to them!***

Meanwhile back in Houston, I learned of a position at an all night convenience story just two blocks away from my apartment. The manager said he'd hire me immediately and pay me more than what I was making in the warehouse. Graveyard shift was a snap. I was to find out that very interesting people come out late at night! Insomniacs have a tendency to hang around when you have work to do because they want to "talk." Early morning commuters want everything yesterday because they are in a hurry. Then, there are the misfits who have no home to go to so they attempt to stick around for security purposes. There were the "five finger discounters" who will rob you blind, if you let them! I learned the routine quickly and was offered Assistant Managership. ***Awareness is the key to survival.***

A fellow named Barry dropped by and we hit it off immediately. He invited me over to his Grandmother's house where he had a room. We sat and watched TV and drank beers. He rolled a "joint" and handed it to me. I lit the "dooby" and inhaled deeply. I was "off" in less than thirty seconds. It was "good stuff!" We became fast friends. His truck broke down one evening, and he needed a ride to pick up more "weed." I kindly obliged. We arrived at Raoul's house some three miles away. He seemed a bit nervous when he first saw me. I still had short hair and was clean-shaven. We talked as he rolled a "joint." He took Barry's word for it that I was not a Narcotics Officer. A month went by and an offer was made to me: "You want to pick up some quick money?" I shrugged and nodded yes. He asked if I knew where Jensen and Lyons streets were. I answered, "Yes." He said, "I need somebody to drop off some packages around there. Are you willing?" I said, "Sure, but ain't that a black area?" He said, "Oh, don't worry, you'll get paid well. Besides, they don't bother us. We have what they want." Raoul snickered as we shook on the deal.

A couple of days later, I got a call from Raoul to come over. He gave me a number six paper bag filled with what looked like small tinfoil envelopes. He told me to stop off at the barbecue stand just north of Lyons and wait. I arrived about seven that evening and sat inside feeling uncomfortable as I was the only white person there. A very attractive girl approached me and said, "You John?" I answered, "Yes." She motioned for me to follow her. We entered a run down government housing project apartment behind the store. Two black males stood up. One reached for the bag, and I pulled it back. One of them said, "It's cool. We got the stuff." I nodded. He passed me a paper bag and the switch was on. I arrived back at Raoul's house where he counted the money. It was all there. He nodded and slipped me a hundred-dollar bill. Within two weeks, I was no longer working at the convenience store. I was making "rounds" all over the Bottoms of Fifth Ward. I had become a "mule" delivering Columbian Flake (power cocaine). It did not register until years later that I had become what I loved riding when I was six years old [mule]! I didn't know it, but I allowed my humanity to leave me. I became an animal, in many ways.

Time passed and new schemes arrived to make more money. I found myself in Galveston, Texas at a wharf. Sealed crates left on a boat were readied for shipping. In exchange, more flake came into Houston. The operations fanned out and became more complicated. There were no more straight up deliveries as before. Another fellow and I rode around in an old car. We had a large ice chest in the trunk. We'd use a portable scale to weigh the Drum and Red Fish we were apparently selling at specific locations in the Bottoms. Girls would come by and slip money in our hands for our product. Inside the fish's mouths were carefully wrapped packets. All of this was done to throw off any scent if sniffed by "narcotics dogs." Nobody, but nobody bothered us! In those days, powder cocaine went for over $1000 a gram.

A guy named Terrell came on board. He made trips west by bus. I'd pick him up in the Heights and take him downtown. I began to notice the same cars following for long distances. I mentioned this to Raoul. He said to not worry about it. One evening he and I went over off Fulton Ave. to pick up a large garbage bag. The elderly couple seemed very pleased to see us. The next night they were on the news! They had been picked up for selling massive quantities of marijuana from an eighteen-wheeler! I packed up whatever I could carry in my car and moved elsewhere to what I thought would be anonymity. Within four days, my new apartment was sacked. Pistol, stash and money were gone. One of my old partners arrived and acted surprised at the theft. Problem was, I hadn't told anybody where I had moved to! The last I heard, Raoul had disappeared. Barry died of lung cancer. Terrell was shot. Tom was hiding out in Louisiana due to a contract on his life. ! It was the grace of God, I wasn't killed, or arrested! ***When we forget God, the first thing to go in our lives is integrity.***

Chapter Seven
Madame Butterfly

Finding a job in Houston in the mid-seventies was never a problem. It was a boomtown based mainly on oil production and refinement into several different by-products. My life was to change with the advent of a new position at Jefferson Davis Hospital on Allen Parkway. Because of my past military service, which was connected to medical training, I took a position in their Labor and Delivery Department! We didn't just deliver babies. No, if one were to look in wastebaskets in each delivery room, he or she might see the remains of tiny hands and feet. They were known as DNCs. I had become a team member in taking as well as giving life. I hadn't thought that much about it. My rationale was: Well the mother may be ill, maybe she was raped, the fetus is already dead or the ultimate lie – I'm helping them reach Heaven quicker.

I was the only white med tech on the unit. Everyone else was African American and mostly female nurses. Needless to say, breaks and lunch time were very interesting. I did my best to mimic a clam, but they were relentless wanting to know how and why I was there. I explained my military service and the fact that I had aided in deliveries of several Korean infants, which we were not supposed to do.

Legalities! Peasant women would limp to the Main Gate of the base and hunch down. Desperate Air Police would call the dispensary begging someone to come out and help the women in labor. We would hop in a "cracker box" (ambulance) and high tail it for the scene. We'd leave American soil, pick up the females and drive out of sight of military eyes to deliver the babies. This I related to the nurses and others who sat in amazement. Slowly, I became part of a team earning grudging respect.

Due to shortages in the Paraplegic Ward, I gladly transferred out of L&D. There were too many of those tiny hands and feet. I worked with specialists and did my thing. The care of massive head injury cases where they become paralyzed is extensive. They must be turned often otherwise bed sores will develop. One case involved a late twenties white male who flipped a motorcycle. He developed an ulcer that went from surface skin to his right pelvic bone. I faithfully cleaned his wound and turned him. Another case involved a thirties something black male with gunshot that nicked his heart. I had gone in to take vitals and suddenly he simply went limp. I began CPR and shouted, "Code Blue!" He died due to a ruptured artery in his heart because of the trajectory of the bullet. Another case was my undoing as I was attempting to properly transfer him from bed to wheelchair for therapy. He began to tremor and before I could get him in his chair, the tendons connecting my spine to muscles in my back had been torn. I was in gut wrenching pain with two compressed discs. I ended up on medical leave and all the painkillers I wanted from the doctor. The effect was exactly like the Portaju I used to drink in Korea! Alcohol and opiates began to rule my miserable existence again. I kept thinking of those tiny hands and feet.

It took about a year before my attorney won a settlement for my injuries. Suddenly, my fortunes had changed! I kept a cool head and budgeted myself frugally. Something inside of me was bubbling to the surface. I had been attending a Chinese Pentecostal church by invitation. It was most certainly a different environment than I was used to. They were most enthusiastic. I felt comfortable in Asian culture because of my past military service, so I stuck around.

It was on a Sunday morning when a couple of missionaries from Japan visited the Chinese church. My mind flashed back to my high school years (1965) when I had written to a pen pal living in Yokohama. Her old address flashed in my mind and I wrote it down. I handed it to one of the missionaries, figuring that nothing would come of it. Months went by and I received a letter from my old pen pal. We began writing again regularly and finally agreed to meet in Hawaii in the summer of 1977. We had never laid eyes on each other except by photographs. The combination of tropical breezes, Mai Tais and romantic music took its toll. I was hooked! My fantasy-laden mind saw Cho Cho San – Madam Butterfly. I thought to myself: Now here was a woman I could control, so demur and obedient! I would be king of the castle, and she would serve me! We parted company after a week-and-a-half and agreed to marry in Houston in December after her immigration paperwork had been processed. I *thought* I would be a happy camper. *We think our motives may seem right, but eventually the truth comes out!*

I returned to Houston to prepare a nest for the butterfly. After the trip to Hawaii, money was beginning to run tight. I hustled to get a job. An old friend from my GBC days helped me obtain a job in the land title insurance business. I started running checks and papers out to their branch offices. I, also, recorded all documents down at the Harris County Court House. I became somewhat familiar with the legal system. Eventually, I learned all about microfiche and microfilmed records. I was a natural at the growing library of legal documents since the "platting of leagues of land" in the Republic of Texas way back in the 1840s. Documents concerning slavery appeared now and then. Such and such healthy Negro male with all his teeth is being traded for a plot of ground. In 1977, reading such fair had no emotional effect. My mind set was that of an *unaware racist*. Yes, there is such a phenomenon, as we shall see later on.

December came and she arrived on schedule. We were married on the 17th, 1977 in Pasadena, Texas. The Area Director of a Christian television network officiated! It was a small affair with honored guests attending including an old flame from GBC. We drove off to our little nest. I promised her that we would return to Japan in three years, or less, for an extended honeymoon. I kept

45

my word to her because of the skyrocketing price of gold in the late seventies. I made a killing! I sold nearly a pound of the precious metal three days before the price tumbled leaving many bankrupt.

The trip back to her homeland and meeting her family is another book in itself. Suffice it to say, culture shock was part of the journey that I never forgot. We returned state side and attended church regularly. I tithed which guaranteed a bright future. God was smiling down on us. I didn't touch a drop of alcohol those first three years of marriage, but problems began to arise after the trip to Japan. I had chosen out of politeness to drink at parties in our honor that set off cravings within me! *God sometimes will bless an undeserving one in a partnership because the other innocent party is protected by His divine favor.*

Nightmares began to return. Eventually, I found myself in a Psychologist's office pouring my guts out. There was this rage within that blocked any form of intimacy. Madame Butterfly decided she wanted to work rather than stay at home and feather the nest. I reluctantly gave in and she seemed fulfilled once again. She thrived and moved on to a better position becoming a Purchasing Agent for a large foreign oil conglomerate. I had taken a new position with one of the largest land title insurance businesses in America. I was promoted time and again. We moved to a lovely home choosing to remain in the Houston Heights. We began to collect antiques. We had friends over often. Problem was, it was all a façade. My rage continued to bubble up and finally it overtook me. I found myself in a private psychiatric hospital attempting to express just what was going on in my mind, but to no avail. I was discharged receiving no relief. I continued my downward spiral into the oblivion of alcoholism and drug addiction.

1985 was a year of constant mental anguish. I couldn't sleep. I barely ate and I drank alcohol like a fish. Although church attendance was regular, it seemed to mean nothing. Even God seemed to be against me! Major Depression crept into the inner core of my being. Living became a futile effort even though I had created a successful company creating signs and exhibition booths for businesses selling their wares at conventions. I found myself driving a truck to the Oklahoma State Fair for a friendly foreign nation to set up their booth that I personally designed and built! All that success meant nothing.

June arrived and my mind began to snap. Alcohol wasn't working for me, it seemed to only exacerbate my already desperate condition. Then it happened! I totally lost any form of equilibrium. I vaguely remember writing a note and placing it on the neighbor's mailbox. It simply read: 'Don't let my wife in the house. It will not be a pretty sight." I proceeded to the kitchen and reached for a full liter bottle of Sake (Japanese Rice Wine). Then I went to the bathroom cabinet and grabbed a nearly full bottle of *Pamelor* - an anti-depressant and a half bottle of *Vicodin* (pain killers). All reason went out the window as I swallowed the pills and drank myself silly. I knew the concoction would be deadly. It seemed that in no time at all, I was slowly becoming anesthetized from all my pain. I dozed off on the bed. I knew that eventually my body would go into convulsions, but my mind would be too far-gone to feel or care!

God really was looking out for me that fateful day. Unbeknownst to me, the neighbor had called in sick for work. He came out on his front porch to smoke a cigarette and noticed the note. I had invited him to our church before and he called the Pastor who came running over at breakneck speed. They attempted to gain entrance through the front door. For some reason, I had gotten up and wandered to the living room where I passed out again in the middle of the floor face down. They could see me inside, but the dead bolt lock prevented my salvation! The neighbor ran next door and called emergency personnel. The police arrived first and managed to "jimmy" the lock on the rear door overlooking the patio. The officer opened the front door and let medical technicians in to check my vital signs. I began fighting the ambulance crew that was desperately attempting to save my life. I was leaving this world fast according to all that I was told later! My mind was in a black out!

The next thing that I do remember was being in total sensory deprivation. It was nothingness! And yet, I was fully aware of my being. No normal perceptions existed in this place. I was alone and becoming terribly afraid. It seemed that if I remained there, I would find myself begging for any form of feeling, even fire! I had to get out of there, but how. I was stuck! The sense of separation from everything near and dear became a point of almost unbearable pain. Horror gripped my mind! Hopelessness enveloped me! All of this was within my mind with no exterior sensation. Life had ceased for me.

I was informed later that emergency personnel had to use electroshock to revive my being. My heart had gone into defibrillation. My breathing had ceased due to the chemically depressed state I had placed myself. I learned later while talking to a young Associate Pastor who visited me in yet another psyche ward, it sounded to him like I had been "cast into outer darkness" awaiting a fate worse than death – Hell! We prayed, and somehow I clung on to a thin ray of hope that Jesus Christ really did love even me!

Little did I realize that my religious upbringing was blocking any belief in a loving God? My background was that of evangelical fundamentalism of the most legalistic variety. My mind set was one of hopelessness because no matter what I did, it would never be good enough! I had absolutely no concept of Grace and very little of God's mercy, so I believed. Coupled with the shame, guilt and sense of having been cheated by God in life, faith was nonexistent! Down deep inside, I honestly believed that God had nothing to do with me. I had become an Agnostic without realizing it. Not until 1990 would new concepts enter my mind that truly rocketed me into a dimension of living that I had never experienced before. I had to hit bottom, so I would look up to see a caring God that had been there in spite of me all along!

Physical pain began to take its toll in my body, especially my feet. Our family physician diagnosed me with Gout. No one in his or her right mind would ever desire to feel the intense agony that this kidney related disease brings on. It is very much like someone driving a white-hot nail through the joints of the victim's body. Razor sharp crystals of purine that is supposed to be filtered out of the body through the kidneys forms in joints, especially lower extremities. The doctor prescribed codeine based painkillers.

Needless to say, it helped with the pain but shades of my old days being hooked on opium came back post haste. By the beginning of 1989, I was no longer fit to work anywhere. I basically became a couch potato watching television endlessly and washing *Vicodin 7.5* tablets down with any form of alcohol I could find in the house. It was not unusual for me to experience incontinence. I simply lost the ability to care about anything, or anybody. Voices began talking to me from the refrigerator motor! I could hear singing from the air conditioner in the bedroom. I was losing my mind, fast!

My condition deteriorated until I found myself in the family doctor's office in December of 1989. He had taken a series of X-rays of my internal organs. I sat there and listened as he explained what I was looking at on the film. The normal liver will show up as light gray. Fatty tissues show up almost as clear spots. Fibrosis shows up as dark gray, or black linear strands. Cirrhosis shows up as almost solidly black nodular splotches. My liver consisted of 15% gray, about 15% fat, 25% dark gray and the rest was just plain black! He asked me if I ever had hepatitis. I answered negatively. He asked if I drank. I retorted, "Every now and then. But, not that much." Then he asked if I ever took acetaminophen for pain. I said, "You mean like Tylenol?" He nodded yes. I answered, "Yes, I used to down them years ago at parties along with other stuff." He winced and said, "What other stuff?" I said, "Does it matter? It was years ago." He said, "It might. What have you taken over the years?" I paused and then began to rattle off a virtual <u>Physician's Desk Reference</u> of various "controlled substances." He then asked, "Did you take any other drugs?" I replied with a question, "You mean illegal stuff?" I nodded my head affirmatively. He said, "What, John?" I mumbled, "Cocaine, heroine, opium, met amphetamines, LSD, peyote, Thai sticks, buttons, marijuana gold, Kona, brown, red..." He waved his hand and said, "I got the picture." There was a pause and then he asked, "And, how much did you say you drank?" I looked puzzled and shrugged my shoulders, "Like anybody else..." I paused and realized I had no idea just how much I was consuming! He said, "What's wrong?" I said sheepishly, "How much alcohol? I don't

know. I can't remember." His expression was of deep sadness.
He pointed at the X-ray and began to explain the concept of drug
interaction. The usage of acetaminophen with alcohol is a deadly
combination. It creates keytones, which are highly toxic and will
literally eat away at healthy liver tissue creating Cirrhosis and
eventual shut down of the organ. He paused and said, "John, I
checked with a specialist. He said you have a year, maybe two, to
live. Your liver is at least a quarter larger than it should be. He
explained how it grows to attempt to compensate for loss by other
means. He then said, "If, and I do mean if, you stop all alcohol
and drug usage immediately, you may live longer. I'm sorry,
John. If I had known earlier, I would have never put you on the
Vicodins. He gave me the number for a drug rehabilitation unit at
a nearby hospital. He made me call while I was in his presence,
which I really resented. I spoke with a Psychiatrist who explained
the basis of their program that were something called the Twelve
Steps. I agreed to go into treatment in early February. He asked
me to put the doctor back on the line. They talked briefly. The
doctor wrote out another prescription for more *Vicodins*. He
called the pharmacy and explained the large amount. I could
feel my face becoming much like a shriveled prune. He turned
to me and said, "You can wait until February 2nd of next year and
take what I prescribe, or find another doctor. You get no more of
these. They'll have to last you until then." I nodded my head and
took the script and said, "Just how much time?" He spoke with a
lowered voice, "I don't know. You're out of my hands." I walked
out of his office stunned. My wife had been waiting and knew
that something was wrong. I simply couldn't talk. She called the
doctor from home and I shall never forget her words, "He can't
be that bad!" ***Denial mocks every member of a dysfunctional
addictive family.***

Chapter Eight
The Turning Point

The Friday I entered the hospital was gray and over cast. It was February 2nd, 1990 – Ground Hog Day. A light rain fell just enough to leave spots on my wife's automobile windshield. She drove up to the entrance and I climbed out. I waved her off and went inside to register for treatment. The Admissions Clerk was matter of fact. An orderly arrived with a wheel chair. Off we went, down several corridors, into an elevator and up to the fourth floor. I was summarily dumped in front of the nurse's station. Eventually, another clerk took vitals and walked me into the doctor's office. She arrived soon after and began her examination. When she touched the upper right quadrant of my abdominal area - my liver area – I winced. She pushed harder and I let out a yell. She asked, "Have you been drinking recently?" I nodded affirmatively. She shook her head and said, "Didn't your doctor tell you not to drink?" I nodded again. I retorted, "It wasn't that much though." She said, "Mr. Keating." She stopped and went on with her exam. She never finished what she was going to say. She left the room momentarily. She returned with an orange pill and a small cup of water. I took it and asked, "What's this?" She said, "Methadone, Mr. Keating. You'll be receiving it for the next five days. Each day we will decrease the dosage until you are stabilized. You will also be receiving muscle relaxants just in case.

If you feel very anxious, we have something for that as well for the next few days. Welcome to treatment, Mr. Keating." She left abruptly. As a Counselor, I know exactly what she was silently thinking back then. "Rationalization!" *Self can be the most destructive force in a person's life if not checked with humility on a regular basis.*

Treatment was an eye opener for me, eventually. I took to it like a duck takes to water until I found out that the water was deeper than I imagined. The Twelve Steps of Recovery were a snap! Each patient was expected to get a Sponsor, have at least five Supporters, call at least three people a day, read pages from what they called a Big Book and attend groups - in house - then go to meetings in the evenings by van. Other than that, we had nothing to do-except counseling sessions. They kept us busy which was the whole idea. "Don't think, just do!" That was their motto.

My first review was a rousing success until my Counselor spoke up. The Review Team consisted of a Psychiatrist, a Medical Doctor, two Registered Nurses, and all Counseling Staff – there were two on board. They asked questions about how I was progressing. I proudly said, "I have three Sponsors, twenty-seven supporters, called at least fifteen people a day, worked the first three steps in four hours, and went to the Sandbox Group at Noon plus all my evening meetings!" There was this long pause. My Counselor leaned forward and very sternly said, "Who are you trying to impress, Mr. Keating?" I stammered, "What do you mean?" He stated, "You were given clear instructions on what to do and when to do it. Why didn't you follow those instructions?" I didn't have an answer. He leaned back in his chair and said, "Mr. Keating, drugs and alcohol are only symptoms of deeper problems. We see patients all the time and most do the absolute minimum to get by, but you, you just had to show everybody how good you are! Why?" I still didn't have an answer. The Psychiatrist said, "Sir, you'll probably make thirty days sober, if you're lucky." He paused. Then said, "Our program is designed in the simplest possible terms. Over achievers rarely make it. They tend to know it all and miss the essence of what it's all about. Slow down. We want you to make it. You're excused, Sir." Later, I went to my

Counselor and told him that I really wanted to make it. I said, "I'll do anything!" He shook his head and said, "That's the problem!" He asked me about my childhood. I began to share matter of factly. He said, "Dig deeper!" There was this generalized physical pain that came over me. I sat there and tears began to trickle down my cheeks. I talked about how I always felt left out. I never fit anywhere. I shared about being left alone at home. Then, it hit me! The criticism from my adoptive mother was almost a daily constant. I blurted out, "No matter how well I did in school, or whatever, that bitch never said I was okay! Nothing was ever good enough! Damn it!" He asked, "What about your father?" I said, "He wasn't there!" He asked, "Who raised you?" I began to feel nauseous at that question. I whispered, "My grand parents." He said, "Who was the alcoholic?" I said, "Carl was." He asked, "Why do you call him Carl?" I began to shake uncontrollably. He said, "Do you need to stop? You don't have to say anything you don't want to. It's okay, and YOU are okay! I'm proud of you." I began to feel myself numbing out. I shut down emotionally, just like I always had done when anyone got too close. I had to be in control, and I didn't have a clue why! He said with a smile on his face, "There's an excellent therapist on the west side when you're ready. He gave me her card as I rose to leave his office, silently. It occurred to me later that no one had ever said they were proud of me before. I pondered my motives for over achieving and decided to use just one Sponsor.

One of the hazards of drug and alcohol withdrawal is sleeplessness. The patient's nerves are shattered; time differentials become much like jet lag; and, emotions are on the edge because the anesthesia of drugs is no longer there. Feelings return, usually guilt, remorse and self-loathing. I was no different than most others on the unit. Pacing the floor in the wee hours of the morning became a ritual. I'd talk with the night nurse who seemed very understanding indeed. She said she had a few relatives that had problems themselves with chemical dependency. She was a Licensed Vocational Nurse who decided to return to school to become registered. She had attended Prairie View A & M Nursing School in the medical center. Yes, she was African American and one of the few black, nursing students at Houston Baptist University.

God moves in strange ways! I mention her at this juncture for a specific reason. Let's fast forward to early 1996 where I was a student studying for a Master of Arts in Counseling. And yes, "PV" is a historically black university founded in the 1870s under the Reconstruction Era. Anyway, I was walking toward the new Education Building when I notice this young lady in hospital greens wearing a white coat. She was feverishly cramming for a test that day. Something said to help her out. I sat down and inquired if I could ask her questions, explain terms, or whatever. She looked at me and cocked her head to one side and said, "Please! I had to work last night and didn't get a chance to study!"

We spent about half an hour reviewing and just helping her relax. I noticed the emblem on her coat pocket, which was where I had gone through treatment six years before. I said, "I think I know you. Did you work on the drug and alcohol treatment unit back in 1990?" She looked at me and kind of squinted her eyes. Suddenly, as if she had a major Gestalt, she exclaimed, "Yes! I remember you. February, 1990!" We shared briefly how each was doing. She went to her class and I to mine. She did pass the exam, and yes, she found me to say thanks. The point is this: What goes around; really does come back around! Today, she is a Psychiatric Registered Nurse and I'm a retired Counselor. We both met our personal bests! And, I am grateful to have had a small part in her success because she certainly had a large part in mine. Now, back to my story.

Treatment had ended and Aftercare lay in my immediate future. There was a large encounter group that met on Friday nights. It consisted of former patients from my treatment unit and another center from Third Ward. We were white and they were all African Americans. We had insurance. They were state sponsored. We didn't have a "problem." They knew we were "the problem!" I was to learn later that this group was a pilot program under a special government grant to mix the two socio-economic groups together. We didn't know it, but the white clients were what African Americans should strive for economically, and we were supposed to get some gratitude because we had not experienced their woes! Well, at least that was the scenario! Little did I realize I was experiencing my future? The very people I scorned would become the object of more love from my heart to theirs than anyone can possibly imagine. A very wise and loving God was setting me up even while I was in treatment.

One incident is worth noting. The Friday night meeting was heated and one of the "brothers" from the other treatment facility brought up the subject of race. Our group of whites began to become squeamish. Eventually, one of the other side looked at me and said, "I want to hear from this white boy over there." The group facilitator corrected him on what he had called me and then nodded in my direction. What came out of my mouth surprised even me! I said, "I don't know. I don't understand. But, I'm willing to learn." I had been taught in treatment that my recovery begins when I take that humble attitude in all my affairs. The brother seemed surprised at my answer. He had been disarmed by an attitude of open-mindedness and honesty. A sister chimed in and looked at me saying, "You ain't like the others. You be real. I love you for that!" After the session ended, the brother came over and shook my hand. He simply said, "All right." I would learn what that meant in years to come, and repeat it everyday often.

Aftercare ended and I moved on to what is known as the Heights Group. It was a hodgepodge of various socio-economic members. The founders were all white and older. There was the blue-collar set and then there were the office people. All had one thing in common, Alcoholism. There was another group that came from a treatment center about five blocks away. A local African American Baptist church had set it up for women with drug and alcohol problems. Ninety percent were black. They'd come in as a mass of talkative humanity dead set on dropping pretenses and staying sober by any means necessary. A number of them asked me to Sponsor them, but my Sponsor said, "Keep your distance. You'd be asking for more trouble than you can handle." Men are supposed to sponsor men and women help women to avoid romantic entanglements. I complied with my Sponsor's suggestion. I really wanted to stay focused on recovery. Besides, I didn't need females calling me at home because my wife and I were having difficulties enough.

The home front had become increasingly tense. I attended AA meetings seven days a week - sometimes twice a day. I really wanted to stay sober. I gained many good friends who seemed to care about me as being worth saving. Often times their words seemed harsh, but I knew they were right. My wife, on the other hand, began to complain about me going to all those meetings. She couldn't see how they were helping me stay off alcohol and other drugs. She had gone through lessons while I was in treatment explaining how the entire family is affected by addiction. She knew the tragic results of alcoholism from her own experience in Japan. Her older brother who had been a promising businessman succumbed to the bottle and ultimately died of diabetes. And yet, she refused to meet me halfway and attend specialized meetings for the relatives and friends of alcoholics so they could be set free from their emotional hurts. Our marriage was beginning to end although it would limp along for almost three more years.

One of the things that I had been confronted with was the fact that I had never really finished anything in my life. I was a great starter and sometimes a good middle person, but finishes did not happen for me. I had begun the convention booth business, but due to my drinking, it waned. I started a lawn care business and it flourished, but again, failure slapped me in the face. Defeat seemed to be my middle name. Then the Twelve Steps came into my life. Character defects that used to keep me down began to be stripped away slowly, but surely. I was becoming freer from the wreckage of my past.

Therapy came my way as I continued to dig into all that was hindering me. Finally, I found myself balled up in a fetal position hugging a Teddy Bear. I lay on a sofa forming a wet spot as tears flowed from my eyes. I could physically feel the torment of what Carl had done to me. I felt dirty, low down and just plain ashamed. As the past came over me in waves, the therapist kept saying, "It's not about anything you have done wrong. He was sick. What he did was not your fault. Let it out, John!" I began to scream and shake my fists. It seemed as if my entire being was coming apart.

This went on for nearly an hour. Every nerve in me seemed to be on fire, especially where injury had occurred. As I raised myself from the sofa, there was this tremendous feeling of release. The sessions were not over by any means. I had to come to terms with Carl's sickness and finally let it go through forgiveness. It was not possible for me to confront him because he had died. I did write a letter to him and read it to the therapist with passion. Then it was time to verbally say, "I forgive." At that very moment, I experienced true freedom. Joyful tears rolled down my eyes. I left her office a real person for the first time in my life. *It's not God's fault that bad things happen to people! He loves us enough to give us free will. What we do with that gift not only affects ourselves but everyone around us. Be careful that you do not take His gifts for granted!*

In 1991, I decided to finish something I had begun year's prior – going back to college. The drive into that Baptist university was very humbling to say the least. I spoke with the Assistant Dean and came clean as to why I had failed three times before after I transferred from GBC. Alcohol and other chemicals had taken their toll of my mental abilities to retain knowledge back then. The life of the streets replaced academia. I asked if I might have one more chance. He thought for a while and said, "John, I am a Christian above all else. I'll see what I can do. I suggest that you take just one course and see how you do with that. Summer semester is starting soon. If you can pull your Grade Point Average up to a 2.0, we'll let you continue." What I had learned from the Twelve Steps was paying off handsomely. *Humility is the key to gaining God's favor coupled with a large dose of obedience.*

The semester began and I met my new Advisor, Jeraldene Dollar. She had years of experience as a Masters Level Social Worker. Her resume was filled with accolades from some of the best organizations in the Greater Houston Area. She knew her stuff! Due to her urging, I switched one of my majors from Sociology to Social Work. Classes began and my life was about to change. Little did I realize that summer would be the turning point for me! My world would become black. Eventually, I would love

57

every moment of it! ***God's ways and thoughts are higher than ours. Like the old gospel song says, "Trust and obey."***

My new attitude had gained me much by the end of the summer semester. Not only did I earn a respectable 3.0 for the course, I gained new friends. My Grade Point Average had risen to 2.0! My most pleasant surprise was the fact that I was not the only "late bloomer" going to college. The average age of collegians had risen in the past fifteen years. More and more middle aged persons were returning to brush up on their skills for continued job promotions. One classmate was in her late sixties. Her family had long since moved out and her spouse had passed on. She felt a need to continue to contribute more to others. What she desired to do was become a Social Worker and that required at least a bachelor's degree. Amazingly enough, I fit right in at age forty-four!

The fall semester arrived and I signed up for a full load. My Advisor had taken a liking to me. We would sit under this tree out behind one of the education buildings and smoke cigarettes and talk. She said the wanted me to be the best Social Worker around. She began to enlighten me about African Americans! She told me things that most white folks would never know in a thousand years. She began to unload a wealth of knowledge. New terms came into my life, like "Redbone, Cinnamon, Chocolate, Yellow, Bright, Good Hair, Bad Hair, and Bee Bees." She laid forth truths about what European Americans had done, not just in the past, but its continuance today! She in no way intended to impart a "guilt trip" within my mind; she was preparing me for my future. ***God really does move in strange ways!***

Being a full time student in any college or university becomes a life style unto itself. Rushing between classes, studying at libraries, doing exacting reports and the real booger – cramming for tests is the routine! There are times when you think your mind cannot take any more knowledge in, but it can! I once heard a minister say, "It's not how much faith you have. It's your confidence in the outcome that matters." That is so true. My attitude of not knowing, nor understanding and asking questions opened the door to everything I would need in the years to come. Little did I realize the track God had placed me on would lead to a dichotomy of "joy and pain." I would learn why "the caged bird can sing." God was setting me free, little by little. I was coming home to my "spiritual roots" and I didn't even know it! Today, they are the only ones that really matter! *Trust God and clean your "house" – answers will come!*

Time passed quickly. My nose was in books constantly. On the home front, my wife had not a clue what I was going through. She went to her job and I worked part-time with a twelve-hour load at school. Pressure was mounting. Something had to give in the relationship. A power struggle for control began to emerge. I was beginning to reassert my manhood. She had become used to a weak-dependent "pet boy" that she could basically order around whenever for whatever. The relationship had become co-dependent. I lost the war of the genders. She loved the power. Her power depended upon my acquiescence. I had become dependent upon her income. It was like two dominoes that had been leaning against one another. One stands up. If the other chooses not to, it will fall! My wife could not see that she too had problems. Sex became non-existent. Despite her increasing resistance, I had a dream of finishing what I had begun - no matter what! *A double-minded man receives nothing from God!*

My Advisor and mentor in Social Work kept the pressure on me. She wanted me to be the very best! We kept meeting under the tree. She did her best to get me to enroll at one of Houston's premier universities. I hesitated because there were no student loans available for what she wanted me to enter, namely the Master's Program of Social Work. There was something inside of me that was going on that was pulling me in another direction. I didn't know exactly what it was, but I knew I had to follow it.

A fellow student befriended me at HBU. His name was Coddie. He was originally from the Watts District of Los Angeles. He went to Rice University on a football scholarship. His future appeared to be the "pros." Without warning, he had an encounter with Christ Jesus that changed his life. He ultimately transferred to take up seminary school! He found the One that supersedes anything on this earth. He had taken the same Social Work course that I had attended in the summer session. At first, we didn't hit it off. He's black and was judging me by the color of my skin. But, as he listened to me in the class, his attitude changed. Eventually, he asked me for a cup of coffee in the Student Union Building. As we communicated, he learned that we had many similarities. We became fast friends. He went on to graduate the semester before me. But, he left me with an open invitation to come visit his church. Almost two years would pass before I saw him again there at the largest minority SBC church in Houston! Yes, the very same one I left before finding St. James Church!

Coddie left me with a gift that became apparent just before I graduated from school. I was sitting in what is known as Weekly Convocation. It was Black History Month. The African American students were in charge of the various meeting programs. There was a special guest by the name of Bernard Jackson who came to the podium. He began to play the meanest saxophone I've ever heard. The "brother" got down with hard-core gospel. The next thing I knew, tears were rolling down my cheeks. What flashed in my mind was my childhood caregiver - Eula. I hadn't thought of her in over forty years. I slowly rose to my feet and began to clap to the rhyme. I couldn't help myself!

The end of the program came and Brother Jackson looked around the gymnasium where the meeting was held. He paused, and for some reason, he looked straight at me! Everyone was standing. He said, "If you know Jesus, sit down." As God is my Judge, my knees wouldn't bend. I tried to sit, it just wasn't happening! I stood there feeling like a fool! Then he said very quietly and simply, "Come forward." I looked down and my feet were moving. I thought to myself, "Oh my God, what am I doing?" I ended up right in front of him. He said, "I'm going to say the Sinner's Prayer. Repeat after me." My mouth opened and the words came out. It's like I had no control! What happened next blew my mind!

As he was leading the very small group of three or four that did come forward, I began to feel hands all over the back of me. There were voices behind me saying, "Thank you, Jesus! Bless him, Lord! Show him the Way!" The prayer ended and I turned to be seated. Much to my surprise, over twenty black students and one Chinese fellow had come up to pray for me and give me hugs! I found out that Coddie, who had been the Black Student's Organization President, had made a special prayer request for this "short four-eyed white boy who needs Jesus." It was the beginning of my road into what I call the "blackness." Unbeknownst to me, my life, aspirations and future were not my own. A seed that had been planted nearly forty years before on a black woman's knee was beginning to be watered.

Graduation came and I faced an uncertain future. I continued to attend AA meetings, but home was becoming increasingly a point of contention. I began attending another anonymous group having to do with sexual addictions. More than anything else, it was a matter of curiosity. What I got from the group was that I was not sexually addicted, but I might need to attend a new group pertaining to relationships. I learned of how some people due to the way they are raised become either Avoidant Addicts or Love Addicts. There were specific behaviors that they do to keep the "psychological dance" that they perform alive and kicking. Eventually, I learned that I had avoidant tendencies. I would get into relationships; begin feeling smothered by enmeshment; and, begin to back out slowly at first. I shut down emotionally which is exactly what I had done with my wife. I learned that Avoidents usually use drugs and alcohol to kill their feelings of guilt for wanting to leave these relationships. This group began to trigger deep-seated emotions that I was not aware were there. Therapy was in my near future.

The Therapist was a middle-aged female who had a Doctorate in Psychology. Fortunately, I was covered by my wife's company insurance so sessions were basically free. The office was plush and in a ritzy part of Houston. She began by asking me pertinent questions about my childhood. All seemed well for the first two sessions. I may have shed a tear or two and even sniffled. The third session came and she switched tactics, which threw me off emotional balance. She wanted to be more specific about the caregiver before Eula. I told her that she was a female with slight Asian features. She began to probe deeper and asked me to relax. I focused on her voice as my eyes slowly closed. The next thing

I knew, I was laying in a fetal position on the sofa in front of her. She asked me how I felt. I replied, "Okay." She asked, "Do you remember anything about your childhood caregiver we just spoke of?" I said, "Yes, she was the wife of a Native American missionary. They were visiting our home. Everyone went out to visit the church except the woman and me. She had volunteered to 'baby sit'." I sat there stunned at what came flying out of my mouth like a bolt of lightening! She wanted to play "doctor." She chose me as the physician. I shall not go into what happened next. I was five years old and didn't have a clue as to the perverseness of her actions. She was the "authority figure" and just like any other child, I accepted her requests because I thought them right! Her physical features had been ***imprinted*** in my young mind.

The therapist and I began to examine the woman's actions and how they had affected my life. Why did I marry an Asian female? She was not the first! I recalled the Hawaiian Princess and the fact that we had almost married. I recounted my antics while stationed in Korea. Those actions were only re-enforcing what was driving me through my "acting out" sexually. My marriage was based on what had fixed itself in my mind at age five because of the sickness of someone else. My relationship with my wife and every other Asian female was a combination of love and hate. Something had to give.

The sessions continued beyond the ten originally agreed to by the insurance company. The therapist referred me to a Psychiatrist who prescribed *Buspar*. It's a non-habit forming anti-anxiety medication. I returned to her office and we continued to work - on me! We dug deeper into my psyche. There was much more to my issues going on all the way back to my first year of life! Abuse, starvation, neglect and ultimate abandonment became subjects of discussion. Then, we came back to when I was twelve. Carl, my adoptive mother's father, became our next subject of examination. What had he done? What effects did it have on me? Not just then, but at that moment in the therapist's office. Tears flowed and I found myself in another fetal position hugging a Teddy Bear at age forty-six! I began to scream! I thought my mind was going to disintegrate. I could physically feel what had happened so many years before. I just wanted the pain to stop. Wave after wave of horrendous terror struck me. I don't honestly know how long I lay there. Eventually, it began to subside and I slowly rose to a sitting position. The therapist gave me a washcloth. I was covered with sweat from brow to chin. I looked down at the Teddy Bear. It had an arm missing! Sometime during the episode, I begun to tear at it in blind rage.

The therapist told me to take two *Buspar,* times three, for the next three days. If I had any unusual dreams or physical manifestations, I was to call her or the Psychiatrist immediately! Sure enough, I did. I shall not elaborate on those, but they nearly ripped me apart inside at one point. My wife just sat and looked at me as if I were crazy. I began to feel anger against her as well. I knew it wasn't her fault, but still the ***association*** between her and my early caregiver was there. Something inside of me knew the marriage was over. It wasn't her fault and that's what made that process so painful when it finally went down. I had to learn to "survive" on my own, if ever I was to become a real man. We finally separated soon after my therapy ended. We did remain friends and continued to talk on the telephone. As a direct result of our separation, she sought therapy and attended a Twelve-Step meeting for co-dependent people. I shall never forget our last conversation. She thanked me for being "man" enough to walk away and make her look within! Both dominoes were learning to stand, but not together! Those seventeen years of marriage were not a waste. Truth is, there were good times. And I am very grateful for those. I can honestly state that I have no animosity, and no regrets. It takes what it takes to get us where we need to be. The secret is in letting go and trusting a loving God that cares so very much for all of us! ***Worms become butterflies, eventually!***

My move to an efficiency apartment was not very far from where my ex-wife and I had resided for years. It was six blocks away. I loved the Houston Heights, which is today an Historic Designated Area. I had taken some pots and pans with me and began to purchase what I might need. I worked at night in the security industry until an opening appeared in Social Work that I could live with. Many jobs are grueling, especially when it involves Child

Protective Services. Something inside of me just wasn't ready to see and experience such trauma. I was still healing from my own past and the ensuing therapy sessions. My new surroundings left me alone to face ME! I began building a another N-scale model railroad. It had houses, roads, an oil tank farm, tiny trucks and cars. It had everything I could dream of! I hand made scaled trees! It became an obsession of sorts. The train I had been denied in childhood and finally earned was gone forever, but I learned a very important lesson: **It's never too late to have a happy childhood!** Yes, you'll see those words along with a Teddy Bear imprinted on what is known as the Survivor's T-shirt. I'm not ashamed to wear it, and I'm age 58 presently. I had survived! I lived to tell about it with no pain, just tremendous gratitude. Those childhood traumas became my greatest assets as a Counselor a few short years later!

What to do with myself became a cumbersome task. I was still attending the relationship meetings on Thursday nights before going on to work. They had become old hat until "she" walked into the room. She was strikingly beautiful, thirties something and an always smiling female with dark wavy hair and the most beautiful light brown skin I had ever seen. She had these dark brown, sparkling eyes and the whitest teeth imaginable. She asked to share the textbook that the group was reading which indicated that she was indeed there for help. She sat three seats away. The group was in a circle. I did my best to stay focused but the perfume she was wearing was getting to me. She was wearing this layered, thin-strapped evening dress and had on spiked heels. I was leading the group that evening. When the meeting was over, She asked me for my name and telephone number. This girl was a "brick house" and all of the blocks were in place! I kindly obliged and thought no more about it until about three days later. The phone rang and this unfamiliar voice began to speak, "Hi John! Remember me? You know, from the meeting Thursday evening?" She began to relate how she appreciated what I had said in the meeting and looked forward to seeing me again, soon. There was a long pause and I said, "There's another meeting on Saturday mornings on the Westside of Houston." She said that she would see me there. I asked her if she was doing well. She said she had a few problems and that we might get together sometime over coffee to talk. I said, "Okay, but I work at nights and need a little shut eye." She said she understood and the conversation ended. I noticed my heart rate had speeded-up, as had my hormones!

Saturday morning was a killer for me as I had worked the night before, but I didn't want to miss this meeting. It wasn't because it was so interesting, but I just wanted to see if SHE would. Sure enough, a vision of loveliness sauntered into the circle. SHE sat down next to me and whispered in my ear, "It's so good to see you, John!" I smiled through my tired bloodshot eyes. With the meeting over, we walked outside to where, coincidentally, her car was parked next to mine. I found out later that she had waited after the other meeting to check out my wheels, or was it the license plate! No! It couldn't be that, could it?

Three weeks of meetings had gone by and we agreed to do that coffee thing. We laughed and joked. I do admit looking to see if there was any ring or indentations from one. There were none! I thought to myself, "That's a good sign." She loved to reach over and touch me when making points during her speaking. I remembered what my Social Work Professor had told me about some cultures where touching is the norm. Finally, I asked the vision of beauty what her ethnicity was. She didn't recognize the term, so I broke it down into one simple word – race. She leaned forward revealing cleavage and very coyly said, "I'm black. I'm originally from Louisiana. Some of my kinfolks are lighter than you!" She began to speak what sounded like French. She informed me that it was Creole. I was intrigued by her charm, good looks and culture – after all, I was a seeker of truth! *A person can justify their way into hell in a hand basket, if you let them!*

We continued to see each other. She began to relate her "mistakes" in life – namely lovers that she had had. She said that what she really longed for was a healthy relationship with a good man. I was in her target cross hairs and didn't realize just how serious she had become. We met one weekday morning for breakfast. She had dropped her two children off at parochial school. She was Catholic. How remarkable! Suddenly, I was Catholic again! We talked of being sexual which she seemed

65

willing to indulge in with me. A motel "just happened" to be next to the restaurant we were breakfasting at. I mentioned I really hadn't thought about bringing any "protection." She said she understood because she had stated she had made a "few mistakes" in her past. We ended our randeveaux in an embrace and kiss in the parking lot. I left for my apartment and she went home. We agreed to meet again in a couple of days. There's a song from the seventies about a Mrs. Jones that comes to mind about now. The fact that she may be married did not compute. After all, I had checked her finger! Sure!

Work was interesting that night. A dear friend of mine named Ben had been cluing me in on "black women", or so I thought. He was a brother and seemed well versed in their ways. He asked me what she and I talked about. I said, "Pretty much everything!"
He says, "Like what?"
I began to relate conversations on various subjects we had passed the time away discussing.
He raised his hand and said, "Wait a minute! She's telling you about her 'mistakes'?"
I said, "Yes, and there's more!"
He shook his head and said, "John, why would any woman, especially a 'sister', tell you everything about herself?"
I really hadn't thought about it that much. It was an infatuation thing, or so I thought.
He asked, "John, how do you really feel about her?"
My answer, "She's a dream come true. If you could see her, you'd know what I mean. She's beautiful."
He says, "You didn't answer my question, John. How do you feel about her?"
I paused and said, "I guess I love her."
He shook his head and blurted out, "John, she's head over heels in love with you. You have to decide how you really feel before she has to 'think'."
I must have looked puzzled.
He continued, "John, when a black woman is really serious about a man she has to think about it."
I must have looked like an idiot!

He looked at me very hard and studying my face as he asked, "John, have you ever dated a black woman before?"
I replied, "Does a one night stand count?"
He says, "No! We're talking relationships here, John."
He kept repeating my name in every sentence. He wanted my full attention.
He said, "What has she told you about her kids. You said she has two, right?"
I answered in the affirmative.
He asked, "And, where did you say she lives?"
I told him the subdivision.
He says, "And, she's not working?"
I answered by nodding my head yes.
He instructed me to ask her about what her home life is like. He then said, "After that, you've got to decide whether it's a go or not. Then she's going to 'think' for a while and you won't see her. You won't hear from her. You'll be hanging high and dry."

The sister and I met the next morning for coffee. We still hadn't become sexual as yet. I inquired as to what her home life was like. That's when she laid a bombshell. She paused and looked at me very carefully. She then said, "John, I sleep in my own bedroom. He sleeps in his. We haven't had sex in over two years. He's a rage-a-holic."

"He works all the time and comes home angry. He takes it out on me and the kids that he didn't finish college. He blames me because I got pregnant and we had to get married. I don't love him. He's my biggest mistake! I swear, John, I was going to tell you! Please don't be angry with me." Tears began to well up in her beautiful dark brown eyes. I sat there half stunned and half feeling her pain. Finally, I said, "It doesn't make any difference, I love you." Fantasyland had struck <u>again</u>!

We continued to see each other almost every morning. We agreed we would wait ninety days so we could both be tested accurately before consummating anything, sexually. She said she was going to start divorce proceedings. I received a call from her one evening before I was about to go to work. She simply said, "I can't see you for a while. I'm sorry. I have to think about all this.

It's so fast." The phone clicked and I remembered Ben's words. Fortunately, he was on duty that night. After I finished my rounds, we talked. He just smiled and said, "Brother, if she comes back, you're in for the ride of you life!"

Three, then four weeks went by. Ben watched me closely. He'd ask me, "How you doing, Bro?" He no longer called me John, for obvious reasons. He figured I was earning my wings as a brother. Little did I realize!

I asked him one evening, "How long does this 'thinking thing' last?"

He chuckled and said, "As long as it takes her."

I said, "A month? Two months? Three?"

He shrugged his shoulders and said, "I waited over a year before my wife made her decision."

I said, "Say what?" I must have looked shocked because he came back with the best line I ever heard. "When a black woman decides she really wants you, it's for life unless you abuse her. She'll walk through hell for you. She'll take a bullet for you. You become her 'man' and that's it! You have a true friend for life. She'll be worth the wait. Just hang in there, man."

I then asked another question after a short statement, "Okay, so I wait. What if she decides that she doesn't want you, then what?"

He looked at me carefully and said, "You'll never see her again."

I must have been frowning at his statement when he retorted, "You did say that her husband had abused her and the kids?"

I said, "Well yes. Do you think she'd lie about that? You know, an excuse."

He shook his head no and said, "I just have a feeling it won't be much longer."

My retort, "Why?"

He said, "Think about it. She's unhappy. Her kids may not be safe. She's looking for a good man, just like she said. You're prime USDA meat! She'll get the house and probably the car in the divorce. She's looking for an employed man with a future to settle down with. You're going to school at PV soon, right?"

I nodded in the affirmative.

Ben says, "It won't be long. Trust me on that one."

She showed up at a Thursday evening meeting. She deliberately sat as far away from me as possible. She had two other people with her – a younger female and what appeared to be her husband. I was to find out later that it was her younger sister! I didn't approach her; nor did I even acknowledge her presence. Yes, I was leading the meeting that evening. They left before the meeting was over so there was no chance for any words.

Ben just smiled when I told him the news. He said, "It won't be long now, brother!"

Sure enough, the next Saturday morning meeting came and she showed up. Did she ever! She had her hair fixed. Her make up was absolutely perfect. She was wearing a black leather sport jacket with just enough cleavage to catch my eye. She had on a tight black skirt, black stockings and those spiked heels. I almost swallowed my tongue. She deliberately sat across the circle from me. Her eyes never left mine. The minutes ticked away. It seemed like forever! We closed with the Lord's Prayer, after all, it was a Twelve Step Group, and we slowly gravitated toward one another. I took her hand and we went outside to our cars. Her full lips had the taste of strawberry. Oh yes, it was on! Two months had passed by. She said she had a birthday party for one of her children; otherwise, she wanted to come by my place for a while. She opened her palm. A condom lay within her hand. She gave me a coy smile and said, "I know we agreed to wait ninety days, but I just want to reward you for being so good to me!" Her eyes welled up with tears as she placed her arms around my neck in a tight embrace. She whispered, "I love you so much." My hormones kicked in big time. It was very difficult to get any rest that day before my evening shift.

Work seemed to be worth it for a change. I had a reason to hustle just a little bit faster. There was a reward for all my efforts in the form of a ready-made family. A beautiful woman that loved me had promised her heart. Could any man ask for more? Yet, there was something about this that troubled me. Yes, my hormones were driving me nuts. Yes, everything seemed to be fine, but there was this gnawing in the pit of my stomach. She had invited a friend to come with her on Thursday evenings to the meetings. The friend had a mouth like a drunken sailor. She seemed arrogant. I finally pulled her to the side and asked what she did for a living. Her answer stunned me.

She said, "I'm a Voodoo Priestess. I'm here to make your love complete."

I said nothing. I just silently walked out of the meeting room to my car in shock.

Ben came in a little late. Although he was an excellent mechanic, he had car trouble himself that night. He stopped to get a new alternator. I covered for him while he secretly replaced the defective one. He came in and washed off in the security office. I began to relate what had happened. He looked at me with the mirror image of how I felt – stunned. He paused and rubbed his chin. Ben then slowly said, "John, you need to get away from her and the priestess. That ain't nothing to fool with. Those people are just plain evil. It will only lead to more heartbreak than you can possibly imagine. I know you said you loved her, but this makes it a whole new ball game. Sorry, man." I nodded my head in the affirmative and made my decision right then. I had to say farewell by any means necessary. That was it for me!

Calling her was not an option. I chose to wait until Thursday evening when I would see her at the meeting. Sure enough, she showed up with the priestess. They sat opposite me in the group circle. She seemed to know that something was up. The close of the session came and I went outside and waited. Eventually, she came out with her "friend." I asked to speak with her alone. She nodded and we walked a few feet away from "the menace." My words were short and to the point. I simply stated that I knew about the priestess and her errant belief in voodoo. I told her that the relationship was over. She just stood there stunned. My car drove from the parking lot and she was still frozen as I left the drive. Yes, it hurt. But, I told myself it would hurt much more if I had chosen to stay in such a sick relationship. I had learned a very important lesson that night. I could say no and mean it! ***Time does not heal all wounds; willingness to change circumstances does!***

Work has a way of helping to bury one's feelings if a person is so inclined. Just as things seemed to come back to normal, another interesting circumstance arose. A brother who worked for one of the companies in the complex began dropping by the security office almost every night. He seemed a friendly sort and loved to talk about his church. Finally, I asked him what church he attended. He rattled off the name, and at first, it didn't register. Then suddenly, like a bolt of lightening, I asked if he knew a Coddie. His eyes became perfectly round as he inquired as to how I knew him. I replied that we attended school together. He grabbed my hand and said, "Brother, you've got to come to church Sunday. Coddie will be there. I'm sure he'll be glad to see you." I nodded my head in the affirmative and told him that I would attend. It was on!

Sunday morning rolled around and I left my post to return to home just long enough to clean up and get rolling again. I followed the directions that had been given to me. Much to my surprise, I had to park almost a quarter of a mile from the church along the road. The place was packed out! It seemed there were people on top of each other. I hadn't thought about the ethnicity of the church until I walked across the parking lot. Everyone there was black with the exception of yours truly. I ran into the co-worker, and he said Coddie was teaching a class and would be out momentarily. Sure enough, there he was coming out of the side entrance. His eyes met mine and we gave each other a big hug. Coddie was a full foot taller than I and the hug was somewhat uneven, but that did not matter. I had seen my old friend from school again. He informed me that he was headed for a satellite ministry to preach, but would look for me the next Sunday in church. I agreed!

The worker led me into the main sanctuary and sat me on the front row. People began to flood the area. It seemed like a sardine festival crammed into one large tin. The band cranked up a rousing song and the choir pitched in. Everybody was clapping and praising the Lord. The Pastor and his Seconds arrived on the stage. My God, I had never seen such enthusiasm in my life. People were shouting and jumping up and down. I just stood there in amazement. Something inside of me said to let go and enjoy the moment. My hands began to clap. My feet began to tap. I swear

I could feel a little wiggle in my hindquarters! One thing I had learned to do, thanks to the Twelve Step programs, was to let go and let God in. That's just what happened. I thoroughly enjoyed myself.

The next Sunday came and I returned for more enthusiasm. It didn't seem to matter that I stuck out like a sore thumb - color wise. I chose to be there. I couldn't explain it at that moment, but it seemed as if I had somehow found an "emotional home." The vast majority of the members I came in contact with didn't seem to mind my presence. They were there for their own reasons, and I was to yet find mine. A couple of ladies began to sit within voice range each Sunday. Both were attractive and always had a warm greeting for me. Eventually, one of them asked if she might sit next to me as someone else had taken her seat. I kindly obliged. We introduced ourselves in polite form. She seemed a bit nervous, but kept looking at me with quick glances during that service. At the end, she said she'd love to be my "friend", if I so chose. I nodded in the affirmative. I should add that the population of the church was about three to one in favor of the females. Little did I realize what that truly meant until years later when I lived and worked in Third Ward and then Fifth Ward! Both areas are almost completely African American.

The Worship Leader asked for those who wanted to accept Jesus or join the church to come forward each service. I took it as matter of fact at first. Then, one Sunday something inside seemed to nudge me forward. I left my seat and proceeded down the isle. Several people began to clap wildly. The church had its first white member! Little did I realize that would be the many of several firsts for me, not just there but throughout the African American community? God had placed me on a track that I never dreamed possible. My life was turning black although my exterior would never change. In time, I would discover the true meaning of the "blackness."

To become a church member meant going through a six-week course on subjects ranging from Salvation, Baptism, and Communion to the Church's history in general and specifically that entity. I sat with other new members who seemed surprised

that I knew so much about Christianity. I explained that I had
attended three years of Bible College in years past. The leader was
cordial and things proceeded nicely. The choir director arrived
one Sunday and asked if anyone had any experience singing in
choirs. He looked directly at me and asked the question again.
I nodded my head yes. He inquired as to where that might be. I
explained that my high school choir had won Ohio State finals
for that division. He smiled and asked if I might be interested in
joining the choir. I politely declined for obvious reasons – color!
He seemed to understand my predicament and quietly left our
gathering. I was to learn that my self-esteem needed bolstering
in weeks to come. Color really wasn't the issue. It was how I saw
myself that was. The damage from my childhood traumas ran
deeper than I imagined, as I was to find out.

   Work continued as usual. I kept going to the relationship
group on Thursday nights. The female and her voodoo priestess
friend had long since gone. I became a regular fixture at church.
A thirties something light complexion female befriended me in
the membership class. She gave me her telephone number and
we began to talk on a regular basis. She was originally from
Alabama. She related how when she was growing up, the other
girls in her all black segregated school made fun of her. She was
called "Miss Bright." The term reflects the almost white color
of the skin thus the saying, "Light, bright and almost white." It
is a cruel joke that darker African Americans say to those that
are lighter. I was beginning to discover that the subject of race
was not just an issue involving the so-called three main races
of Mongoloid, Negroid and Caucasoid. Oh no, it runs much,
much deeper. Discrimination and even genocide occurs within
racial groups all too frequently. Idi Amin is a perfect example of
racial hatred in Uganda years ago before his exile and ultimate
death. All participants were African, but subtle differences
made for mass murder on a grand scale. Northern Ireland is
another example of the madness. Protestants killing Catholics
and the reverse over a land that can support both parties, if
only they chose to look beyond their differences. Actually, it's
more complicated than just forgetting. It's a desire to celebrate

the differences as issues that can enhance and make life more beautiful for all, like in the salad bowl example.

We continued to become fast friends. I learned that she was an Instructor at Prairie View A & M University! I had a vague vision of what it was from snippets on television from time to time. I knew that it was a predominantly black school and little else. She seemed to think I would like going there for a Master of Arts in Counseling. I was given contact numbers and who to see! I was on my way to the experience of my life! That joy and pain thing was coming my way one more time! I was going deeper into the "blackness."

Chapter Nine
The Only Constant Is Change

The Fall Semester was beginning at "The Hill". Prairie
View A & M University is affectionately called that by students
and faculty alike. If you go toward the water tower, you will
understand why the name. It is the only "hill" in a broad grassy
covered plain called "prairie." My first visit impressed me beyond
my wildest mental visions. Perhaps, my "learned" racist ideas
of what a Historically Black College should look like clouded
what I was to find was a very beautiful reality. Many views and
beliefs that I held so dear and believed to be so very true were to
be changed forever. As one person said so many years ago which
still stands true today: "A lie never lasts!" God was with me from
the very start at "PV." One other thing that ultimately came to
my realization in due time was the fact that I was being watched.
Under the circumstances, it is perfectly understandable, but I did
not know that at the time!

Long registration lines became my first test of endurance.
Some students, mostly the younger ones, seemed to have an
"attitude" when they saw my complexion. Others did not seem to
care one way or the other. They just wanted to get the registration
phase over with. Still others were very friendly indeed. Color
and a false sense of superiority shaded my views of those long
lines – not to mention the people about me. Who was I to expect

that I should always be first in anything? The concept of "white privilege" was an accepted fact of life for me. I took it for granted that I should be first everywhere! Suddenly, reality was slapping me up side my hard head – I wasn't squat at PV. I was just another haggard student scampering from one class to the next. Another expectation that warped my own faulty belief system was that I honestly believed that I would have to work harder to get good grades because I was white at a black college. I expected reverse discrimination! I just knew the Professors would have it in for me. Little did I realize that is exactly the feeling black students have at predominantly white universities! Not only that, I learned that I was eligible for a Reverse Minority Scholarship! Why? You guessed it – it is that white thing again! Life had flipped for this short four-eyed white boy. My mind kept thinking, "Oh my God, what have I gotten myself into?" Truth is, I was getting my first bitter morsels of what it means to be black in a white racist America. My views would radically change in years to come, and I am so very grateful for that change today!

My work at the security job continued which supported my school efforts. Each Saturday morning another officer came in fifteen minutes early so I could make the forty some odd mile trek up US 290 to PV. I would arrive just in the nick of time, run into my first class and wheeze as I seated myself before the Instructor arrived. The class was on Group Counseling Techniques. The Instructor seemed to have no use for me at first, but as time passed, he noticed that I was sharing my notes with other students. He learned that I helped others cram for quizzes and tests. What I had learned in those Twelve Step meetings about helping others was paying off handsomely. This short four-eyed white boy was making friends. School became a passion. I spent hours in the ornate library studying over scientific data on all sorts of subjects. I accessed the Federal Information Repository on the Web. The Texas A & M Library Reserve was also at my beck and call. Learn instead of burn was my motto!

Students would come up to me from God only knows where and begin asking if I could help them. They invariably said that someone I knew sent them because they knew I had all the answers. They may have been partially right because at the end of my first semester, I had a 4.0 grade point average. However, I did not see it that way! What I was feeling was tremendous pressure from having to appear perfect! I began to realize that there was something going on here that was not right. Suddenly, a question had to be asked, not of me, but other students! Why do you – as black students – expect me as a white student to be so perfect? I pulled a "sister" about my age to the side and asked her the question about perfection. She was taken aback for an instant. Then she said after a short pause, "You're right John. Why would I expect you to be better?" We both just sat there on a bench in silence. We both looked at each other simultaneously and experienced a mutual Gestalt: White Privilege and Black Acquiescence! Both groups were going along because it was more convenient than confronting the issue straight on and alleviating the very real problem at hand. In other words, both groups had somehow been hoodwinked and kept the momentum through tradition! The attitude that that's the way it has always been seemed to prevail? I was taking my first look into what makes both ethnithcities tick. It was not a pretty sight. I recalled what Ms. Dollar had taught me about "good hair verses bad hair." Where did that come from? That was a "black thing", so I believed? I thought of the PV Instructor friend who talked about her victimization simply because she was lighter. How deep did this black acquiescence go? *If you want to know a man, walk a mile in his moccasins.*

Counseling is a profession where the therapist may guide, or cajole, the client into finding answers to the problems that already exist within. The techniques may vary from one school of thought to another, but the object is always the same – do no harm to the client and help him or her find their own way. At first, my back rose up very much like a disturbed cat at such a notion. How can someone who is emotionally imbalanced possibly have enough "where with all" to find solutions to their **own** problems? That seemed like a paradox! The very organ – the brain – that has the solution is working against the solution to keep the client off balance. Actually, it is rather simple. Focus on the solution long enough and the mind will follow and find balance again. Focus on the problem and wham – you get a bigger problem leading to more imbalances. Therapy is a skill that has to be honed much like a good knife that must be sharp enough to cut away at the excess fat to get to the good stuff – Prime USDA meat, or the solution! This and much more was being crammed into my cerebellum from classroom to classroom.

On the work front, a new member arrived on board. Her name was Mikki. She was a twenty-seven year old African American female with a very aloof attitude. She definitely would not speak to me at all! She had a thing about white males, as I was to learn. She had been in the US Army and experienced male chauvinism up close and personal. I left her alone except for actual work duties. I thought of what she must have gone through. To be sure, one of the myths that white males in particular believe is that all black women are sexually "easy." In other words, they are more than willing to oblige in exchange for favors. It's called "something something" in the hood. More of that racist stereotyping that plagues sisters, and sexism against women in general regardless of ethnicity. Truth is, the brunt of sexual harassment has been against black women for as long as this country has existed. Therefore, I respected Mikki at a distance because I had knowledge of her general history. I wanted to remain proud of me by practicing principals that gave me a clear conscience and sleep filled nights.

In due time, duties changed at the post and I ended up doing Mikki's job once a week, so we had to converse about what to expect on the shift and any procedural changes. She had to ask me about mine that I shared freely to make the "switch" as easy as possible for her. She reciprocated. She saw that I backed off of any sexist comments and gave her "respectful space." She came to realize that I was not attempting to "hit" on her. Eventually, we began to converse about outside interests. I learned that she had a four-year-old son, and yes, a "man." As we both let down our defenses, I further learned that her man was unemployed; and, basically hanging around the house not looking for employment while consuming the groceries she was bringing home on her meager salary. On top of those burdens, Mikki was attending business school in the mornings while her "man" baby-sat. This girl had it going on! She was like a little bulldog, and cute as a button. She got to the point where she would smile at me in front of the group at shift change and say, "Strong black woman!" I would reply, "You go girl!" She knew where I was going to school and was very inquisitive about my studies. I would share and do my best to encourage her to "hang in there" at her school.

It was a stormy evening and the security truck that Mikki drove had broken down. She sat in the security office with me. I was behind the computerized monitors that observed almost every angle of entry and exit on to the large complex. She was reading one of my textbooks. She asked me about raising children. I said, "I didn't know that much because I didn't breed well in captivity." It took her a moment to get the joke. Then she said, "How sad. No kids!" I looked at her chocolate face covered by horned rimmed round-lens glasses. She did what has been called the "neck thing" that only a black woman can pull off correctly. It's like shifting the head to one side while keeping it level in a quick staccato motion that extends the neck in an S shape from shoulders to head. It is her way of letting you know something is up. It may be good! It may be bad! It is one of those signals that most "brothers" secretly fear.

I studied her face momentarily and said, "It's not necessarily sad that I don't have kids. It is a choice I made many years ago. I was a practicing alcoholic and drug addict back then. I hated myself and certainly didn't want another me running round in this world."

Mikki shook her head and said, "But, haven't you ever wanted to have a baby?"

I was in a playful mood and replied, "That would be extremely painful. I'm not built for it!"

She brushed my comment aside and studied my face intently. She was serious about my loss. At least, in her mind, my not having progeny was a loss. It is a cultural thing, as I was to learn soon enough. She felt very strongly that the race had to carry on no matter what. She then said the words that was to nearly blow my mind, "John, you're a good man. You are not an addict now! I'd be willing to have a baby for you." I almost fell out of my seat.

I righted myself and leaned forward and said, ""You what?" She looked into my eyes more intensely than before, "Yes, I would. Definitely!" There was a long silence from both of us. Our eyes did not move from each other's. The sun was beginning to rise and that night's shift was almost over. She said, "You want to go have breakfast when we get off shift?" I said, "Hey, I only have two bucks. I will cash a check today and we will do it tomorrow morning. Is that cool with you?" She smiled and said, "Okay, big boy!" She started to reach out and touch my shoulder and pulled her hand back quickly. A coy smile came on her face, which made my night complete.

The next morning turned out to be very interesting indeed. It seemed that her sister had experienced "car troubles" and needed a quick lift over to a nearby store where she worked as a clerk. Mikki asked me if I would run her from our post to her work place. I looked at her and started to say, "But, I thought we…" I experienced "the hand" for the very first time. She didn't want to hear my whining. Her sister needed a ride and blew off the breakfast appointment!

TIME OUT! For those of you who have not received the dreaded "hand," you are in for a treat. We have discussed the "neck thing" already. There is another signal that you simply do not want to mess with. It called the "dreaded hand." When a black woman doesn't want to hear any more of your crap, she whips her wrist up and snaps the hand in an upright position with the palm out, usually in your face! If you are wise, you will immediately seek a position of alert silence. She means business. If you continue to talk, or whatever else she deems unnecessary, you will receive the obligatory, "Excuse me?" This is really not a question and is stated in a sarcastic tone. She is in actuality warning you to back off, NOW! Only a fool would continue to attempt any further communication. She is done with whatever it is. That's it! She is leaving your foolishness to you. She doesn't want to hear it – period!

Mikki had given me the hand. I dutifully drove her sister a few blocks away to her job site. She smiled and made light conversation. She asked me questions about school, and what I wanted to do with my life. She seemed impressed and wished me all the best as we pulled up in front of the store. She climbed out and told me, "You get back to Mikki, hear?" I nodded and drove back to the office. Mikki had disappeared! I thought to myself, "Rats! I'll eat breakfast alone." Ultimately, I decided to just go home and have a glass of warm milk to lull myself into dreamland. What else was new, I had become accustomed to living alone again after seventeen years of marriage. That was not an easy chore. Yet, for some reason, I felt lonely that morning as I drove home.

The next night's shift came all too quickly. I had forgotten that it was Mikki's day off. I was still feeling a bit "miffed" because it seemed that she had broken her word about having breakfast the morning before. My duties went as usual until about ten o'clock that evening. I received a radio message from Ben to report to the main office immediately. He informed me that I had two guests waiting. I began scratching my head and wondering who would want to see me at that hour while I was on duty. Other fellow workers I hung with, a few fellow students I studied with and a couple of sisters from church that I knew came to mind. My size seven shoes rushed me over to see who it might be. I entered the office and a young male child was sitting in the small lobby area next to Ben. I had to admit that he was indeed one of the cutest kids I'd ever seen. The little tike's name was Damitrius as I was to learn. He looked up at me with perfectly big brown eyes and threw his arms out wide. I gave him a hug, and tickled his tummy. He was absolutely delighted. He stood up in the chair and shouted in his pajamas, "I'm a Man!" Ben and I broke out laughing. I looked up and Mikki had returned from the "facilities" and had been watching the exchange between Damitrius and myself. She had this big smile on her face, and I swear her eyes were twinkling. She came over beside me and placed her hand on top of mine that was resting on the front counter by that time. She inquired, "What do you think of him?" I said that I thought he was a truly beautiful little boy. I asked if his dad was at home. She dryly said, he's not Damitrius's father. Nothing else was said on that matter. We talked briefly about work and just things in general, as the little guy began to doze off. Mikki said she would see me tomorrow and we would talk then. She drove off and Ben said to me, "John, she like's you a lot. She is a real keeper! A friend for life, if you know what I mean?" I said nothing and returned to my duties elsewhere in the complex. I was thinking of the last relationship and the pain that it gave me. I was determined to move slowly on everything, except my studies.

The next night at work was uneventful. I was walking from one building to another to check a door alarm, which was not uncommon. Mikki pulled up in the patrol vehicle. I hopped in and we took off. She sat outside while I used my coded security zip card to enter. I found that one of the late night cleaning people had left the door ajar in a sensitive area where computer records were stored. I logged in the incident and proceeded back down to the truck. She was listening to a gospel tape that I had loaned her. We headed off for the office to take a short break. I sipped a cup of luke-warm coffee with not enough sugar while Ben observed the television monitors. Mikki came from the rear and we were off. She was supposed to take me over to the third complex building area, but decided to make a detour. She pulled out onto a nearby street where the vehicle would be off cameras momentarily. She stopped halfway and left only the parking lights on. She quietly asked me, "John, how does a Grand Slam Breakfast sound after work? I'm buying." I paused for a moment and replied with a slender smile on my lips, "You're on, sister girl." We drove back to the third building and I got out. I noticed my heart began to race just a bit faster. There was a spring in my steps as I settled in for observation duties in that area for a while. An officer could see two-thirds of the complex from my little hide away on the tenth floor.

Sunrise came and the shift was over. She hopped in her car and I in mine. I followed her as best I could. She was doing almost seventy-five down the West Loop! We turned onto US 59 and exited near a restaurant that remained open all night. We entered and took seats in the rear. She seemed a bit nervous as we chatted quietly about Damitrius and how he was doing. I really liked the little guy. She leaned back and stretched her arms out. She smiled and asked if I liked the view. Although she was in uniform, she had a very inviting figure. She was definitely a woman! She looked down the front of her blouse that almost stretched the buttons to the bursting point. She asked if I knew how much the rooms were across the parking lot at the motel next door. I shrugged my shoulders. She calmly said, "Twenty-four ninety-five for the day. My sister is taking care of Damitrius." I leaned forward and asked her if she really knew what she was doing. She looked puzzled. I then said, "If I didn't care about you, which I really do, we'd be over there in a minute. However, let's take this slow. It's not that I don't want to; I just don't want any complications right now. I have to keep my head on straight. A college education will do more for a possible future for you and Damitrius than a trip next door. Please don't get me wrong, I want to; but can we take this slowly? What do you think?"

There was a long pause as she looked down at the table. I thought she was about to cry. She seemed almost despondent as I asked her, "What's going on behind those beautiful big, brown eyes, Mikki?" She slowly raised her head and said, "You must think I'm a slut!" Her eyes quickly met mine and I reached for her hand. I very softly said, "If that were the case, we wouldn't be sitting her talking right now. We'd be over there screwing. I'm just saying that I care enough about you and Damitrius to do the right thing by you two. Yes, I do care for you. You are an exciting woman to be with. You're funny. What I really like most of all is that in spite of all the crap that's gone down in your life, you have hung in there and are getting an education for yourself. I'm very proud of you, girl!" A tear rolled down her chocolate brown cheek. She made no effort to wipe it off. What came out of my mouth next surprised even me, "Mikki. You once said you'd be willing to have a baby for me. I really do feel honored that you would feel that way, but what I'd much rather prefer is a baby with you when the time is right. Think about it, okay?" She shrugged her shoulders and looked away. She was still smarting from what she saw as my rejection of her physical appeal. There was nothing I could do about that.

We went to breakfast the next morning, but it wasn't the same. She had an issue that she wasn't willing to face involving deep-seated shame and probable abuse. Soon after, I was transferred to another post and I didn't see her for almost a year. I received an invitation to her wedding. She settled for the man she had been so unhappy with. I understood. At the reception, I leaned over to give her a gentle kiss on her cheek to say farewell. She turned her face toward me and kissed me on my lips in front of everyone. What I learned from her, I shall never forget as long as I live. She taught me how shame robs people of the best even when it pursues them. She was a wounded and fragile child under the "strong black woman" façade that she wore. Truth is, she's not alone. I've met many since. To be sure, she was and is a very special lady. She had another son soon after her first wedding anniversary. Her husband did finally get a good job and they're still together and happy. That makes me happy, and that's what really matters.

School was going very well. I was cramming for mid-term exams. I had a paper due in Multicultural Counseling. I had chosen the topic of Sexual Abuse by Ethnithicity. I wanted to see if there were any statistical data on this topic. I was surfing the Federal Information Repository and there it was! My eyes could not fathom what I was reading. According to 1995 data, 7% of white females by age 16 had been the victim of rape, incest or molestation. Hispanic females ranked next with 13% becoming victims by age 16. The next statistic blew me away. African American females by age 16 that had been victims of rape, incest or molestation was over 27%! My next question was why was this so high? I began to dig deeper and found a truth that shamed me as a white male.

Fact: The first person hired for a job is not the males in African American culture. It's females. Why? They are perceived as being less of a threat in the work place. By whom? It's none other than the privileged white males who control finance and industry. Coupled with the myth that says these females are "easy" makes for an inviting target. However, these white males are not necessarily the culprits of said sexual offenses. The black males at home are the enraged ones stuck in low paying, dead-end jobs barely eking out a living for themselves, let alone a family. Competition sets in for whatever jobs are available. Who wins?

The females who become the power brokers in the family because they are bringing home the bacon. Eventually, their women resent the men which only perpetuates another myth of the lazy, shiftless black male in her eyes. She buys into the myth. He reacts with Displacement – misplaced anger and violence – at her and the battle is on. Alcohol and other drugs only serve to deaden the pain of his dilemma, and at the same time releases his inhibitions toward brute force. The results are jails, institutions or death for him and single household female providers subject to abuse by any man that enters her world. When all other predicators of manhood are taken away, sexual prowess becomes the only tool left for dominance by any means necessary. I began to understand why Mikki was willing to "jump" at a man with a future even though she had a man at home. She had a child to consider and knew the statistics all too well that are against black men in America.

As I read the data, I almost wept. I could remember times when I had said, "I'm not a racist. I never hurt anybody. Why, some of my best friends are…" The chickens were coming home to roost for me! As that brother from the SBC church said, "John, there's no turning back for you. You know too much!" How true his words were. The only way I can face African Americans today is with a deep sense of humility and deep sadness. Every white person in this nation is guilty of racism. Problem is most are truly unaware of what they have created with over sixty years of welfare programs that do nothing, help no one and make grant-sucking whores out of those who call themselves caregivers.

On the church front, interesting developments were occurring. I was sitting in church one Sunday morning quietly waiting for the service to begin. I noticed a vision of loveliness coming my way. She seemed in a hurry. She was one of the ushers at the time. She came up to me; leaned over and kissed me on the cheek; and then, whispered in my ear, "I love you!" Before I could respond, she had disappeared! I had spoken with her a few times before. She was in her late forties. She was recently divorced with a 27-year-old daughter. She had recently retired from her years of corporate service. She was attending court-reporting school. She was starting a new life and was obviously lonely. I remembered

what Ben had told me once, "John, you're prime USDA meat."
Yes, people were watching me at church – primarily females. At
school it was faculty and students. And at work, co-workers and
the police who we worked with. I was in trouble and didn't know it
at first!

Where I worked at the complex, there was a truly red necked,
pot-bellied police officer that vehemently hated blacks. He learned
that I was attending PV and decided to make my life a living hell.
He called some of his buddies on the force who jammed radio
transmissions, deliberately sprung doors open to set off alarms
and began leaving porno messages with my name attached all over
Houston. He'd come in the security office and make comments
like, "How's our little race traitor today? Or Hey, nigger lover, is
the p---y good?" He was spoiling for a fight - just waitng for me
to react so he could get me fired and even arrested. I learned to
bite my tongue just like African Americans have had to do for
centuries in this race-based society. There was no turning back
for me! I was left with this rage within that could not be easily
quenched. There were times when I'd sit in my apartment and
cry, then scream and then fall asleep out of sheer exhaustion. I
was wearing another man's moccasins and being prepared for the
future.

Graduation was approaching for me. What I had begun in 1991
at Baptist college had continued at PV. I was finishing planned
events for a change. My life appeared to be on track, but where?
Everything seemed to be "peachy" as some would say. Little did
I realize that my life would take another turn leading me deeper
into the "blackness." Misunderstandings arose at the SBC church.
I had become the butt of slander by a small group of members
who wanted me gone by any means necessary. Rather than fight,
I chose to leave temporarily which turned into permanence. I
missed church, but something inside said to move onward. My
divorce was becoming finalized. A new career lay ahead, but
another turn of events was to change my life totally.

Chapter Ten
Finding Eula

I continued to go to meetings at a Twelve-Step group in the Houston Heights. A brother had recently begun attending. He asked if I would be his Sponsor. I agreed. We hit if off and things were going great. He mentioned his old home group and asked if I wanted to come over and visit. I agreed. We drove over to the northeast side of the city to a tiny hole-in-the-wall-meeting place. I found that I was the only white person there! The group consisted of brothers and sisters who were recovering from crack cocaine, primarily. They welcomed me warmly and I truly enjoyed the atmosphere. The socio-economic level was lower than PV or the church that I had left; the culture was essentially the same. I decided to continue going back on an almost daily basis. A deciding factor that made me finally move from the group in the Heights to the northeast side came in the form of my Sponsor.

My white Sponsor's name was Robert. He had blue eyes, blonde hair and a surfer-like tan. He had his own construction company. He dutifully led me through the Twelve Steps of Recovery. He asked if he could speak with me at the meeting hall. I agreed. We sat on a plush sofa and he hesitated for a moment. He then said, "John, you're a bright man [no pun intended]. You've got so much going for you. I mean, you're really smart." He paused and then he continued, "So, why the hell are you attending

Prairie View? And, why are you going to that nigger church? And furthermore, why are you going over to the northeast side with all those God damned darkies?" He was losing control of himself. He stood up and walked in a circle. He sat back down and continued, "You could go to Rice, U of H. Hell, you could go to Harvard or Yale. You're that smart! Why John, why?"

I sat there stunned and smarting from his remarks. I slowly opened my mouth and said, "Well, Robert. Number one. PV is one of the finest universities in the country and I attend on a Reverse Minority Scholarship. Number two. I was invited to that nigger church as you call it, and I really enjoy the worship. Number three. I go over to the northeast side because, if nothing else, I'm getting a sense of gratitude. I could have been strung out on crack! Robert, who made you God of the Universe? According to the third tradition, the only requirement for anyone to be a member of any Twelve-Step group is to want to stop whatever they are doing. And four. It's none of your damn business anyway! And five. You're fired as my Sponsor. Work the steps yourself!" With that said, I calmly walked out and did not return for several weeks. I felt empowered for some reason. I had said and done the right thing. It felt good! I was "living the dream" without realizing it at the time.

My permanent move to become a full-fledged member of the northeast side group was immediate. I began attending meetings daily. I made new friends. I obtained a new Sponsor who I might add used to be a "gangster." My world-view was changing. I listened as people poured out their hearts and souls. I watched tears shed. I truly "felt" their pain. My heart went out to these whom had been the brunt of racism, sexism, classism, and of course, one of the worst conspiracies to strike black society – deliberate drug "dumping." I was falling in love with a culture I used to despise. Little did I realize, I was getting free for the first time in my life. God had placed me in a "problem" for a reason. I was to find out, in time, that I could be a part of a greater solution than I ever dreamed possible!

In the meantime, my uniqueness – the only white male - made for very interesting encounters with the ladies in the group.

Sharilyn was the first to "hit on me." She was willowy and had incredible legs that she seemed to enjoy exhibiting. She already had a fiancee of sorts, but the idea of trying "something different" on the down low proved irresistible. She made it a point to sit next to me during meetings. She'd put her arm around me and gently use her fingers to caress my neck and upper back with gentle circular motions. Truth is, I thoroughly enjoyed her advances. She eventually spoke with me privately in the front parking area one evening. She wanted to know if I'd like to come over to her apartment for coffee. I wisely told her that I'd take a "rain check" on the offer. What I was really considering was the fact that she was already in a relationship, if that's what you want to call it. I had no desire to have any more holes in my body than what the Good Lord had already created!

School was wrapping up at PV. Final exams were approaching and my Master's Thesis had yet to come back from the publisher. The ultimate grade on the thesis had to be 4.0 – no mistakes whatsoever! The pressure was on me to finish up well. I thought of the summer semester in the past year. It was five weeks of pure hell on earth. Statistical Analysis was the course title. The instructor was new and spoke with a heavy Middle Eastern accent. He knew his data, but lacked the finesse to pull off gaining the student's attention. In other words, he was one boring dude!

I walked into class one hectic morning fully ready for a pop quiz that had been announced the prior day. An announced pop quiz? Perhaps our instructor had not a clue as to what the term pop quiz was all about. Oh well! I knew I had a 4.0 GPA. The pressure was tremendous. People have been known to go psychotic under such stress. Marriages ended over the student's desire to excel in education because spouses felt "left out." It occurred to me, "Why am I putting myself through all this for just a few points more, grade wise that is?" The test was passed out and I chose not to answer three questions knowing full well that it would lower my total grade for the course. The grades were posted and yours truly was off the hook! It actually felt great not to be labeled an "egg head." God blessed me with a very respectable final Grade Point Average of 3.84! I found that I could be less than perfect and still be "acceptable" to those about me. I could relax and truly enjoy school and living in general. What a concept! But, for someone who had been told they would never amount to anything – this idea was totally new and a little bit scary at first. **When you realize that God loves you, that's good enough! You cannot get any better than that.**

My graduation was a most rewarding affair. All graduating students lined up according to their chosen field of study. Doctorates went first in the parade of note worthies. Masters level graduates came next; and then, bringing up the rear were the Bachelor Degreed persons. It turned out that the field of Counseling was near the beginning of the procession because of its alphabetical position – the letter C. We sat up front and center on the main floor of what is affectionately known as the "Baby Dome" that is about a quarter the size of the Astrodome in Houston, Texas.

The dignitaries droned on congratulating themselves on their latest discoveries and scientific feats. Finally, it was time for the role call of graduates. We stood and lined up facing stage left. As each name was called out, that person came across the stage to shake the hand of the President, Dean of Students and then receive their diploma. I stood at the foot of the steps leading up to the stage area. Name after name was honored. My name was read and I walked forward, but something happened that stopped the procession cold! There began a series of shouts and hollers. Applause broke out. I quickly glanced out toward the noise. At least two-thirds of the Counseling graduates were on their feet. They were shouting, "You go, John! We love you!" I slowly moved forward, accepted congratulations and walked off the stage to hugs from my peers. No one else received that overt reaction except me that day! But why?

It is said that what goes around comes around. I tend to believe that is a very true statement. Students who already had enough pressure just being black and going to college on top of that, found a short four-eyed white boy who was willing to take the time to help others cram for exams, explain "pyschobabel" and wish them well. They were just saying thanks in their own way on graduation day. And yes, it did leave a very warm place in my heart and fond memories. When I think of that moment today, I almost shed a tear because I chose to go beyond myself for others with no expectation of reward.

There's one more thing I share here that I never mentioned before this book. Prior to graduation, each student had to be fitted for cap and gown. Yes, that was just one more line to endure. I left the Student Union after my fitting and proceeded to my car. I hadn't thought much about it, other than the fact that the price was a bit steep for my lowly student budget, but the gown had to be purchased. Maybe my attitude comes from being what I call "thrifty." Anyway, it came time to pick up my gown, cap and white sash. I walked up to the counter and gave my name. The young lady came back with the goods. I reached for my wallet and then it happened! She said, "Mr. Keating, put it away. It's paid for." I did a double take and reached for the receipt. Sure enough, it was marked PAID! I shrugged my shoulder and then said, "Do you know who that might be?" The student clerk nodded her head no and I was on my way. To this day, I have no idea who did that favor, but God bless you brother or sister! **Wealth has nothing to do with money. It's a heart thing!**

Even though I was carrying a full academic load at PV and working full time at night, I found time to attend Twelve Step meetings, especially the one on relationships. The group consisted of primarily males. I shall never forget one very special evening as I sat and listened intently to a middle-aged white male who was in tears. He attempted to articulate his dilemma. It seems that he had gone through therapy over issues involving relations with his biological mother. They were not close. She worked outside the home – a professional person. Her son was left in the care of a "mammy" – a black female caregiver. The male child was still in late infancy and had not yet been weaned. The caregiver nursed him from her breasts. It seems that the caregiver had left her position with his family and was never seen again. However, an indelible imprint had been placed in the subconscious of this group member's mind. He continued to relate his therapeutic experiences to the group. He said he began to have dreams in his late adulthood about smooth, soft, black skin and the incredible feeling of warmth and security he felt. He said he had these cravings for milk. He would add a bit of sugar to it and didn't know why. He was hypnotized to find the origins of all these dreams and cravings. While under the therapist's trance-like state, the patient acted out sucking motions. His hands were reaching for something, but the therapist knew not what! The patient was brought back into his conscious state and asked if he remembered anything at all. He answered that he did not.

The therapist instructed him to talk with other family members. In doing so, he might find someone who would be able to explain, or trigger, a memory from his past. He spoke with an older sister who related how a black lady had nursed him when he was yet an infant! She told him how she would hold him gently in her arms and sing while giving him nourishment. Unfortunately, his sister couldn't remember the caregiver's name. The group continued to listen as he shared how he became obsessed with finding this lady. He had become a well to do businessman and hired a private investigator to find this early "mother image." Good fortune was not his lot. There seemed to be no trace of her, anywhere!

This man continued to share with the group about his problem. He was sobbing! I sat and watched transfixed on his sad continence. Something began to bubble within me as I felt his very real pain. Somehow, I could identify. He continued to say that he wanted to find her to set up a college fund for African American students in her name! He was grateful for the warmth and tenderness that she had shown him so many years before. He said, "If I could just find someone, somewhere who knew her, I could have peace!" A tear rolled down my cheek. A distant memory that only flickered for a tiny nanosecond when Vernard Johnson played his saxophone was coming into view. Much like a bolt of lightening from out of a bluish-black sky hit me. I shouted, "Eula!" The group looked at me like I had lost my mind. The other male sensed what was happening. He asked, "Are you having memories too?" I nodded in the affirmative and apologized to the group for my outburst. The leader that night said, "No apology needed. That's what this group is for. Healing." The other male who had shared his heart-wrenching story asked, "John, what's going on?"

My mouth quivered as words came tumbling out about a black woman that I had all but forgotten. Her name was Eula, the common-law wife of a black sharecropper named Tom. It seemed like yesterday as memories began to be unlocked from the deep recesses of my mind. Tears flowed as my voice cracked. As some would say, "I was 'slinging snot'." I didn't care, this had to come out. I talked about a mule. I hadn't thought of that old beast of burden since I was six years old! I was forty-eight and desperately wanted to find "home." I shared for almost ten minutes as others watched and listened intently. Two other white males were nodding their heads as the subject of early childhood caregivers came too close to home. We exchanged telephone numbers and went our respective ways.

Days had passed and the telephone rang about dinnertime. It was one of the white males. He asked if he could talk. I told him to wait as I pulled a hot skillet off the stove where a pork chop was cooking. I picked up the receiver and he began telling me that he had made a few calls to other friends of his. He said, "Damn, there are five others like you and me in the group! They had black baby sitters, or live-ins." I said, "You're kidding aren't you?" He exclaimed, "No! I'm for real on this. Have you done anything to find your mammy?" I said, "I thought about it, but it was so long ago. I doubt if I'd be successful. Besides, what would I say? She probably wouldn't remember me anyway." He cut me off in mid sentence, "You'll never know until you try. Go for it, man. I am!" I told him that I'd think about it and get back to him. We said farewell and I went back to my pork chop.

My mind began to think about how I would start such a search for a person I had not seen in forty-two years. It seemed impossible! The odds were definitely against me, and yet, I knew I had to make an attempt at searching for her. I pondered whom I should contact to get suggestions on this project. I remembered programs on afternoon television talk shows where long lost relatives were located and re-united with family that were believed to be dead. Perhaps if I watched one of those, I might get lucky and obtain an address from the credits at the end of the show. Then I dismissed the idea as being foolish. What would be the odds of seeing a television show on the exact topic that interested me when I turned on the tube? Astronomical odds, to say the least. I almost laughed at myself for entertaining such a magical thought. And yet, I reached for the remote control to flip on the television. The picture came on and I began surfing channels. Much to my surprise, a man was talking about finding his twin brother whom he had been separated from since birth! My ears perked up much like a Doberman Pincer on the prowl. The talk show guests told of how he started at the last place they had been together and then go from there. That seemed simple enough. I knew that! It would be the City of Colquitt, Miller County, Georgia was the last place I had seen Eula. So, what next?

The dialing buttons were pressed to the numbers 1-4-1-1. The search began with a kind lady's voice saying, "What city and listing please?" I was admittedly nervous and said, "Colquitt County, Georgia." She repeated, "And what listing sir?" I paused and said the name of the church where my adoptive father had pastored way back then. That seemed logical. The operator dialed the number, and low and behold, a male voice came on the line. He introduced himself and I began to say why I was calling. He very kindly asked me, "Sir, I don't want to offend you, but are you white?" I said, "Yes." The gentleman turned out to be the minister of a church, but not what I was looking for. He seemed to sense my dilemma and asked, "Are you sure you have the right county?" He said, "This is Colquitt County, Georgia." Suddenly, it snapped. I was looking for Colquitt, Georgia as his words came over the line, "There is a Colquitt, Georgia in Miller County. I apologized for inconveniencing him. He said, "I hope you find her." He hung up.

I took a deep breath and tried to not appear like a fool as I requested Colquitt, Georgia this time to Information. In no time at all, I was talking to an operator in that city. I explained that I was looking for...suddenly, I froze up. I knew that calling her a "mammy" was politically incorrect. Times had changed, thank God! How do I explain the relationship to the operator? Just as quickly, I blurted, "I'm looking for my Spiritual mother. Yes, that's it, my Spiritual mother." The operator asked for more information about her. I told her that her name was Eula and that's all I knew at that moment. I knew that she had lived in that area when my family left in 1954. The operator made an excellent suggestion. She gave me the name of the local newspaper editor. I could write a letter that, if I were even half way fortunate, might get me a lead through the paper. I hurriedly wrote down the name and number. The next day, I called the Colquitt, Georgia newspaper. I had to explain my predicament to yet another person. The young lady had a deep Southern accent. I must say that she was very patient with me. I as struggling to keep my emotions in check. I was on a "mission" and I would not be detoured! She referred me to the Editor. I had to re-explain my desire to find Eula. He said, "You know, this sounds like a really interesting story. I'll tell you what Mr. Keating, you write down a letter with what information you have and we'll publish it! Keep in mind, we normally don't do this sort of thing, but this sounds too good to pass over." I obtained his exact name and address. I thanked him very much and disconnected myself from the line.

The next morning started off as usual. I sipped a cup of coffee laced with way too much sugar and French vanilla creamer. The toast crunched between my teeth as I sat down at my computer. How do I explain this to the general public without possibly creating danger for Eula? My memories of how things had been were very vivid. Back in the fifties and sixties, the fellows in white sheets ruled that area with an iron fist. Would there be repercussions if race became a central issue? I said a little prayer and began clicking the keys on my keyboard. The letter was complete in ten minutes! I licked a stamp and drove to the local post office. As I lifted the mail shoot, I placed my fate in the hands of many others.

School and church went on as usual. Life seemed ho hum. I all but forgot my search. Almost two weeks had passed when the telephone rang. I was an unfamiliar voice calling from Colquitt, Georgia. A Mr. Stewart was on the line. He informed me that he had been a Deacon in my Father's church. He said he had wondered whatever had happened to those nice folks from "up North." I was stunned! He talked about the barbecues his family had to raise money for the church. He asked me if I remembered the frog legs jumping in the skillet. He told me I was very amused at the sight! I hadn't remembered, but I took his word for it. I did remember a hole where a pig was being roasted in the pit. He said, "Oh yes, we still do that, but it's on a big iron grill today." Finally, we got to the subject at hand – Eula.

He informed me that Tom had passed on and she had moved in town somewhere. The old sharecropper's house had gone into disrepair and ultimately fell down. The house my family had lived in, next door, had been refurbished and a black family was maintaining forty acres behind their new dwelling. He didn't know who they were, but they seemed nice enough. I asked about the mule. He chuckled and told me a story about that mule. It seems that Tom had left me sitting on the mule's back while he went inside our home to answer a question Eula had made of him. I somehow managed to touch the mule's flank and it began to move! It headed straight for the family's newly budding garden of sweet peas, corn, cabbage, radishes and the like. The mule trampled along moving in a wide circle. Not much was left to say the least! Tom, Eula and my parents came out on the front stoop to find that the mule and I were gone! Eula started shouting at Tom, "Oh Jesus, save Johnny!" About that time, I let out a laugh and the race was on. Everyone came to the garden to stop the mule and rescue its passenger. Tom apologized for the damage, but my Father being the good man he was told him not to worry. Mr. Stewart's words were triggering memories that had been hidden in the deepest recesses of my mind for decades. I recalled what Eula had done when the mule was found. She reached up and plucked me from its haunches. She held me tightly and kissed my forehead. My adoptive mother looked on saying nothing. I don't remember receiving any affection from her, but Eula gave me plenty. Mr. Stewart said he'd check around and see what he could find out.

No sooner than I had hung up the phone than another call came in from East Texas! It seems that a lady who had grown up in Colquitt had moved with her husband to the Big Thicket, which is a heavily wooded area several miles northeast of Houston. She had the Colquitt paper mailed to her each week. She distinctly

remembered my family and me. She recounted her days as a
young girl about my age. She had gone to the church. She said
she thought that Eula had moved to Waycross, Georgia. She
wasn't sure, but she'd check on it for me! I thanked her and we
disconnected.

The next day, I checked my message machine to find that four
other people from the Miller County area had called! I listened
to each caller's voice and decided to answer the one that "sounded
black." [No racial slur intended.] I dialed the number and a
child answered. She seemed to understand the importance of the
call. She screamed that a white man from Houston was calling
about the paper. Within seconds, an adult female voice came on
the line. I identified myself and thanked her for calling with any
information about Eula. She said, "Sir, it's an honor to talk to you.
Everybody's buzzing like bees. This is the first time black and
white folks have talked to each other in a good, long time. How
can I help you, Sir?" I paused and asked the obvious question,
"Where might I find Eula?" She retorted, "You talking about Miss
Anderson whose husband was Tom?" I said, "Well, all I could
remember was her first name and where she lived." She paused
for a moment and said, "I'm pretty sure that's Miss Anderson. She
be in a rest home just outside town." I asked, "Do you have the
number handy, Mam?" She shouted for someone to get her the
phone book. I listened, as she said, "Not that one, the yellow one.
Hurry now, this man's waiting." I could hear pages rustling and
then came the number. I thanked her very much for all her trouble.
She replied, "Ain't no trouble, Sir. God bless ya." She hung up
before I could get her name! I had a number, but I wanted to verify
it before disturbing the wrong person who was "resting."

The next person I spoke with was a young white male whose
father had talked about the Damned Yankees from up north who
came down to Colquitt to change things. He told me that his late
father had been a Klan member. He said in an apologetic tone that
he didn't agree with him. The son had grown up in an integrated
school system. He chuckled and said, "Some of my best friends
are Negroes today." I said nothing and chose to just listen. He
said he vaguely remembered his mother talking about an incident

involving a black man whose wife had been raped. Rumor was that they lynched him at the courthouse for striking a white man with a fireplace poker stick. "There was this white preacher that tried to stop the raucous", he said. "They ran them Yankees out of town", he continued to say. There was a long pause and said, "Oh, I'm sorry." He said he'd ask around about the lady in question and call me back.

My next call went pretty much like the prior one. This time it was a white lady identifying herself as being over sixty years of age. She said she remembered the preacher and his wife. She said the preacher's wife had taught her daughter piano lessons. Her words kicked in a memory of a recital for students that our family had attended so many years ago. It was a balmy evening. The recital was held outside covered with a canopy of stars. Pieces of the puzzle making up my early life were falling into place. She went on to say that she remembered the young black couple that lived just down the road from the Yankee family. She went on to say that the female had taken care of their little boy. She told me that the woman was indeed residing at the Miller County Home for the Aged. She gave me the number, which turned out to be identical from the African American lady who had given it prior. I thanked her so very much for the information and hung up. My next move was to call the "home" and hopefully talk with someone from forty-two years in my past – Eula.

My nerves were on edge as I pressed the telephone keys. Ringing began and a female voice answered the name of the "home." I introduced myself and explained why I was calling. She said, "We've been wondering when you'd call. Miss Eula is sleeping right now, but if you call tomorrow about ten o'clock Eastern Time, we'll make sure you get to talk to her." I thanked her so very much and said I'd call tomorrow. What happened next surprised even me. Tears began to roll down my cheeks. I simply said to myself, "HOME!"

I called up one of the white males that was looking for his "Spiritual mother" as well. He was stunned. He bombarded me with questions on how I had found Eula so quickly. He wanted every possible detail, yesterday! I did my best to oblige him. He stated that he thought I was very fortunate indeed. I was! There are instances of people looking for others for years without a trace. I, on the other hand, had found Eula in a matter of weeks. God was smiling down on me. Little did I realize the impact of the next day's call on my life!

The time was exactly nine o'clock Central Time as I began to push the buttons on my telephone. My hands were shaking as the ringing began. The same lady that had answered the day before came on the line. I identified myself and she said, "Here's Miss Eula." A weak sounding voice came on the line, "Hello, hello." I managed to keep my composure and told her my name. She said, "Oh yes, the preacher's boy, little Johnny." She started talking about how the pigs got out and everybody was chasing them down the dirt road trying to catch them. She talked about how my father had found me playing with a King snake and nearly had a heart attack. She told me about the Sunday go to meetings that they used to have near the swamp behind the back forty. It seems that my father went back to have outdoor church with "those people." She talked about Tom and the mule, and yes, the garden incident. She went on and on. My face was flush and eyes were becoming swollen from rubbing the tears away. No, I was not sad by any means. As my Chinese brothers and sisters say, "I was 'crying happy'."

Finally, there was this long pause and she said again, "Hello, hello. Are you still there Johnny?" I answered, "Yes Mammy, I surely am. It's so good to hear your voice." I then said, "I'm sorry, I shouldn't have called you that." She replied, "That's what you used to call me long time ago. It's all right. I'm glad you called." I broke in and said, "The reason I called was to thank you for what you gave me when I was little. Is there anything I can do for you?" Without hesitation she said, "I could use some money to get my hair fixed. It's so nappy right now. You know what that is don't you?" I answered, "Yes Mam, I do. I'm going to Prairie View A & M University." She inquired, "What's that, a barber college?" She was still thinking in terms of hair. I kept my composure and continued to ask her questions about her life. She told me that she never had much schooling. Her family had to work the fields. She met Tom through a friend. They never "jumped the broomstick", but they loved each other just the same. She paused and I asked, "Did you all have any kids?" There was a long pause and then she shared, "Johnny, I couldn't have babies. But, I loved you and Charles." I asked who he was with a tinge of jealously rising up. Eula stated, "He's a little white boy I took care of after you all left. He sends me money now and then. Can you send me some money? I needs to get my hair fixed. She was starting to repeat herself and I knew that she probably needed rest. She said, "Don't forget, I ain't got much time left." I told her a money order would arrive in about a week. I asked her to take good care of herself. Then I told her that I loved her. She replied, "I know, Johnny." We said our good byes and I made arrangements to speak with her the following Sunday at a pre-arranged time at her convenience. She did receive the money as far as I know. I couldn't make the trek back to Georgia because I was in school and dared not miss sessions. I sent her letters from time to time explaining my life – especially letting her know that Prairie View A & M University was one of the finest institutions of higher learning in America. She ultimately passed on, but she will always live in my heart. When a short little white boy needed love most of all, it came from a black angel named Eula. And, I choose to pass that on...

Chapter Eleven
Care Giving, Death and Creoles

My time at the SBC church had ended. I was firmly linked with the northeast Twelve-Step group. I was working the profession of caregiving. The amount of money I was making was near what I used to earn when I had my own company years prior. My past career was to create booths for exhibits. It was creative work, but there was a problem that came in the form of a bottle. I began to miss appointments. Excuses became out right lies that became a life style. In the end, I lost it all. I was married at that time and my wife took up the slack as I drifted downward into a bottomless pit.

God had given me a second chance at life. As a professional caregiver, I could see the fruits of my labors once again. Lives were being changed for the better. I would go into the field and counsel minority women with children who desperately needed aid. Many of them were battered. Some were pregnant with complications such as HIV/AIDS, Hepatitis B or C. Still others simply needed a bag of groceries to make ends meet until the "eagle screamed." I observed the direct and indirect effects of racism up close and personal. I witnessed the hopelessness in the eyes of women who had loved and lost. Often times, I allowed myself to cry when I left work to "get it out of me."

The most heart wrenching clientele of all were the "crack mothers." I'd sit and listen to the lies of young women whose

bellies were bulging with child inside and know that that little
one may very well be born shivering, shaking and screaming
from the withdrawal of cocaine in its tiny system. I'd refer them
to treatment if at all possible. Most continued to lie and "use." I
learned that life is not so simple in the "hood." Just saying NO is
not enough! Support must be there on a constant basis for many
whose lives have been wrecked by drugs and alcohol. In spite of
the heartache that I witnessed on a daily basis, I loved what I did.
It gave me meaning. I felt useful. I was blessed!

The northeast group meetings continued for me. I had made
friends with a sister whom I must say was and still is strikingly
beautiful. She and I began talking on the telephone on a regular
basis. We began to share from our hearts. We told each other facts
about our lives that no one else would ever know. A bond of trust
and honest affection began to appear. Our relationship was not
sexual. That would have ruined everything. Yes, we had feelings
in that area, but there was something about her that compelled
me to "walk the straight and narrow." We had similar childhood
traumas. And yes, both of us had been involved in prostitution
at one point. I had "used" women to obtain information through
extortion. She had sold herself to make ends meet. We both
had suffered from Major Depression at one point. And, we both
attended the same church – St. James Church. She was the one that
had invited me in the first place. Love began to bloom between us,
but the bigotry of others raised its ugly head and stood in the way.
She was understandably afraid.

People who hate do despicable things in the name of humanity
and even God! My female friend unfortunately listened to the lies
of others and believed what they were saying. She had been told
things about me, or that I said this or that about her that created an
atmosphere of mistrust and bitterness in due time. I sought out a
therapist to face my part in the dilemma. The Counselor suggested
that I leave the northeast side group and find my own way anew. I
concurred. Problem was that the female saw this as abandonment
and she began a campaign of stalking me. Before it was over, I
had learned that she had been arrested for that stalking. Someone
had turned her into the police! There were those who still worked

feverishly to get us back together because they saw something special there. Ultimately, I left St. James in exasperation.

During that heartbreaking period of my life, I had fallen and injured the bottom rib on my right side. X-rays were taken. Then the physician called me and said he wanted to do a complete blood work up known as a spectrum analysis. I came to his office and the sample was drawn. A few days later, his nurse called me up and asked me to return. That day, I shall never forget as long as I live. He showed me the X-rays of my liver. He read off and explained in detail my blood analysis. He told me that I had acute Hepatitis B Virus! He said I should get my affairs in order because I had three to five years to live. This was in March of 1997. He said he was sorry and if I needed anything, to call him day or night. I left his office in total shock.

It seemed that the bottom had fallen out of my life. Emotional pain was all that was left. It seemed that God was not there and not listening to anything I had to say. However, in all that tumult, one miracle had happened. I had not picked up a drink of alcohol or taken any mind-altering drugs. I remained sober! I lost my Counseling position and did odd jobs to stay afloat. Things came to a head after I hit bottom and ended up in a flophouse. A friend suggested that I contact the Administrator of a place called A Better Way, Inc. to see if they might have a counseling position open. It was a halfway house for men. Although I was not a Licensed Chemical Dependency Counselor, the "chief" hired me. I was a lowly "counselor intern," but I had a job and a beautiful apartment courtesy of the establishment! I hadn't given up. I just hung in there!

I packed my small car with my belongings; said farewell to the Fifth Ward of Houston; headed for the Museum District. My new surroundings were palatial compared to what I had just left. I began working the day following my arrival at the halfway house. I loved what I was doing. Again, I could see the fruits of my labor as man after man graduated and went on to be successful, clean and sober fathers, husbands and workers for a change. Life was sweet! But, I had not learned my most important lesson yet. It would not be until 2004 that I came to complete terms with God and myself.

A power struggle began to brew between the new Director of the Halfway house and it's governing body. In the end, the Director was fired. She was a stone cold sister who knew her stuff when it came to drug and alcohol treatment. I supported her completely. The halfway house lost its license to practice under Texas guidelines. Fortunately, the other Counselor had befriended me. He had signed off on my work each day. When the bottom fell out once again, he invited me to come live with him – where else? – back in Fifth Ward! Oh my God! One more time in the "ghetto?"

Yes, HL was as black as you could get. He was a character who had a wry sense of humor. He had more "woman trouble" than a dog has fleas. He drove a small roadster and considered himself to be a "player." For the folks reading this book who do not know the term player, this is it! He is a man who knows how to swoon women into whatever situation he chooses by using his "Mac" – his smooth talking. A player is not a "pimp daddy", but they are first cousins of sorts. Both men use women to get what they want, when they want it.

Fifth Ward is a very large area encompassing most of the northeast quadrant of Houston. It is known for the "Nickel Attitude" – much like the personality of a junkyard dog who's very hungry indeed. Gang warfare is not uncommon. On any given day, ""hos" go "trickin" on corners. They are looking for "johns" to give "licks" to. The money they make from sexual favors goes to buy "rocks" which they smoke in the "stem" to get a "major, " or a "blast." As many say in the hood: "Let me break you off a piece [explain things]." A ho is a prostitute. Trickin is picking up a customer. A john is the customer. A rock is a small piece of crack cocaine. A stem is a form of crack pipe. A major or blast is a really good high. It should be noted that in spite of all the crime, the vast majority of African Americans are honest, hard working, fiercely religious, upstanding citizens in their own right. I know because I've lived their experience. Yes, it is possible for this short four-eyed white boy to live, work and play by their rules in their area. I wouldn't trade those experiences for all the money in the world! Anyway, no one could ask for better neighbors than they.

HL's home was located just north of Lyons Avenue, which is one of the main thoroughfares for commerce. He had somewhat of an eclectic décor including a parachute that draped across the entire living room ceiling. There were Masai warrior spears and Filipino machetes standing erect in one corner near the open-hearth fireplace that was never used. He had books stacked almost everywhere and all of his business papers graced the dinning room table in jumbled masses. He knew where everything was and no one was to touch his "stuff." He was fifty years old when we first met. He looked more like seventy and walked the part. He suffered from arthritis, emphysema, kidney disease and type-one diabetes. In spite of his ailments, he loved to play jokes on others. He was known for his loud colored shirts and ties. He always wore a style cap because he said it kept the glare of the sun out of his eyes. Most importantly, he was my friend – for real!

The reason we took a liking for each other is probably due to the fact that we were opposites in almost every way. The "color thing" was obvious black verses white. He had been a Black Panther back in the sixties. I had been a Goldwater/Nixon Republican. He dressed much like a part-time pimp. I wore very conservative clothing, usually khaki pants and white long-sleeved shirts. He always had extra starch in everything he wore. Creases were extremely important to him. I, on the other hand, looked very much like a crumpled paper bag. He always had something going on almost every night. I was a homebody and die-hard couch potato. But, there's one thing we had in common that made all the differences pale in comparison. We both had mellowed out and had come to terms with the concept of "just getting along."

HL and I talked until the wee hours of the morning about what it means to be black or white in America. He seemed to know by gut level instinct I was for real when it came to the subject of race. He'd say, "You ain't no Mr. Charlie." I remember breaking down and crying in front of him when I heard that a former client of mine had gone into defibrillation after a good hit of crack. He died at age 32 in Third Ward. His family didn't have the money to bury him. He was laid to rest in a particle board box. That's no way for anyone to go. HL consoled me by saying, "He made his own choices. He won't be the last client you'll lose. Get used to it. Yes, it's hard, but all we can do is tell them 'what it is'." I nodded my head in agreement, but it didn't take the pain away. He was right, there would be more senseless deaths from drugs, AIDS, hepatitis and "drive bys." I had entered a world where life was cheap; where if you were a black male over fifty – it became a novelty – a miracle. Parts of me were coming unglued. I began to sense that each time I heard of another death, a little bit of me went with them. I have a theory that when I pass, maybe, just maybe, I'll get those pieces back on the other side. After all, we are all connected by a Higher Power – in my case I call Him, Christ Jesus.

I became employed by the largest recovery center in Houston based in Third Ward. I was still a Counselor Intern, but making more money than before. I worked at the south side facility on Belfort Avenue. The job was tedious and often times exasperating. Clients who went through twenty-eight days of treatment would "flip out" and be using as soon as they left the facility. I had to keep in mind what HL said, "They make choices they must live or die with." I became jaded in time. I worked my tail off and felt that I was losing the war. Kids who were only eighteen came in for treatment and couldn't add two and two anymore because they literally burned out their brains. The terrible cost of being black in a white racist America was all too evident. The rage that began years before continued to grow within me.

I begun attending Twelve Step meetings on the south side of Houston. The environment was decidedly different than the northeast group. The south-siders seemed to be far more serious about their sobriety. There was very little "hustling" going on. By that, I mean looking for sex on the sly, or "down low." I became active and led a number of meetings. Then it happened! SHE walked into the room and caught my eye. She was a vision of loveliness that had a college education – a professional woman! She was very independent and mature. She was forty-eight at the time. She had jet-black curly hair, dark sparkling eyes, a hilarious sense of humor, a figure that was out of this world and the smoothest skin I had ever felt. Her name was Rose.

Rose and I seemed to have an instant rapport from the start. She had the most beautiful smile and what she called "bubble cheeks." Yes, she was slightly plump and her face was round hence the nickname concerning her facial features. She was a bit of a tease when it came to attracting me. She'd begin the hard to get role and flip it to romantic interludes. She was easy to talk with on almost any subject because she truly was very intelligent. She lived with her twenty-one year old son in a two-bedroom apartment in Pasadena, Texas. Her son was struggling to find himself and the product of a single parent household. She had left her husband some seventeen years before due to domestic violence. She moved to Houston to start her life over again. She came with little else than the clothing on her back and a young mouth to feed. I had to admire her tenacity and perseverance. She was a real "trooper."

We began our relationship very cautiously. I'd drive from Fifth Ward all the way to where she lived that was well over twenty miles one-way. I didn't care about the distance. She was worth every mile. We'd have tea and cookies on her front balcony where we'd just sit and talk for hours. Eventually, she invited me over for dinner on a Saturday evening. What a feast it was! I acquired a taste for Creole cuisine. She was from the Mississippi River Delta and spoke fluent Creole that is a form of French with a twang, so to speak. She was Roman Catholic, but only nominally so. She attended Mass infrequently. Her view on the church was different than my own. I was a convert and she had been raised among "knuckle busting" nuns. She felt that the church was overtly racist because there were very few black priests. I tended to agree with her on that point. She was willing to compromise. We attended a charismatic Catholic Church weekly that she seemed to enjoy very much. I simply enjoyed having her by my side wherever we found ourselves in spite of the "looks" that inevitably came our way – a white male and a very dark black female walking along holding hands wherever.

As we continued to bond, we eventually spoke of the "M" word. We even picked out a matching set of rings. We'd play Scrabble on her dinning room table and talk of planning a home and life together. We'd snuggle up and watch rented movies, especially comedies. But there was something that troubled me about her behavior. She would reach over and touch my face and say, "You have such beautiful pink skin." I thanked her, but knew that there was something much deeper to the meaning of her words than complimentary.

Back in the mid nineties I became part of a group known as the Center for the Healing of Racism. The founder – I called her Miss Cherry – was a sister with a passion for seeing black and white people get together in peace with equality. She created a program that was coherent and straight to the point. It consisted of a ten-week course with lessons on everything from stereotyping to unaware racism, from institutional racism to outright genocide. There was no confrontation, only acts of forgiveness after being shown the damage that had been done by the dominant ethnic group against all minority groups, not just black folks. She pointed out where so called good hair versus bad hair mythology came from. She talked about the "paper bag test" that blacks used to keep out darker colored blacks from "speak eases" in New Orleans and elsewhere. Ultimately, the tears flowed from my eyes as I identified my part in the problem and renounced my ethnic upbringing being overtly racist. I truly had not known just how deeply affected other cultures were by the paranoia, willful ignorance and superstitious mythology of the dominant white culture. I suspected that Rose, my Creole Queen, was a victim herself, but I didn't know just how deeply she had been hurt, not so much by whites but by her own family!

Cherry answered the phone at the center and warm greetings were exchanged. I had not talked with her for quite a while. It was so good to hear her voice once again. We caught up on old times and how we were presently. Eventually, we got around to the reason for my call. I related to her how my lady friend was behaving. I told her – in confidence – how she seemed to have this fascination for my pink skin. Cherry listened intently making verbal nods with her voice to let me know that she was truly listening. Finally, I ended with what I believed the problem was – namely that Rose was very dark in complexion and the rest of her family was not. She had mentioned that her younger sister was the favorite. She also mentioned that when Rose was twelve years of age, she was sent to live with her Uncle and Auntie. She never elaborated on why, but I had a suspicion – her dark color brought shame to the family of lighter Creoles. There was also the specter of an erroneous belief about infidelity on behalf of her mother with another man?

Cherry is a very wise person to say the least and she knows her culture all too well. She tended to think that my hunch was right on the money. She also wanted to meet Rose for herself. She informed me that a ten-week dialogue was about to start. She wanted Rose and I to be there, especially for the session on Internalized Racism. Yes, there is such a thing! That's where the minority culture emotionally and even spiritually inculcates the racist values of the majority, or ruling culture. Lighter blacks considered themselves more acceptable and hence superior to darker blacks. Softer, smoother hair is more superior than more brittle, coarse hair. Good verses bad hair made for acceptability. The list goes on including the paper bag test used in the 1920s to exclude blacks from nightclubs that were considered too dark! Such cruelty existed in hopes that the dominant culture might accept at least some of the minority culture. Whites could enter mixed nightclubs at will where lighter blacks collaborated for survival's sake at the expense of their own darker brothers and sisters! That's the madness of racism! It is very much like a disease that we'll delve into later on in this book.

Rose seemed to thoroughly enjoy the first three sessions of the dialogue on racism, then came the next one on Internalized Racism. Cherry asked the group how they had been affected by their "own" who had internalized the disease. A young woman from Fifth Ward related how she and her brother were harassed constantly because they lived in what was known as "French Town." That particular area was primarily populated by lighter skinned Creoles originally from Louisiana. The surrounding area was resided by what she called the "garden variety blacks." Cherry stopped her and asked why she called them that. She said that's what they – the Creoles – called their darker neighbors. And yet, she couldn't see how her label was just as offensive as calling her "light, bright and almost white." I observed Rose as she began to shuffle in her seat. I could tell that she was becoming uncomfortable. Finally, Rose raised her hand and began to unload years of hurt and humiliation about her upbringing. She almost cried as she related how she always felt "less than." I reached over and placed my hand on hers as she continued to let her burden go that she had carried for so long. Cherry looked at me and smiled broadly. What I had done was give my Creole Queen permission to be free from her past by inviting her and then supporting her openly.

Our relationship became even closer. There was nothing that we did not share with each other. We discussed budgets, housing, transportation needs, taxes, recreation and hobbies, religion and even sexual fantasies that we had had. She wanted me to meet her family in Louisiana. We planned on going over on Thanksgiving for a family reunion of sorts. She said she needed to go over on the 13th and 14th of November to get things ready. She wanted to put her mother in a nursing home due to the fact that she suffered from dementia. She also wanted to bring her father back to Houston so he could receive better care at the Veteran's Hospital than in his hometown. I asked her if she wanted me to go along, but she said she would make the trip alone. I reluctantly stayed behind that turned out to be one of the most critical decisions of my life!

Rose had gone with her son back to the "delta." I was left on my own for the weekend. I attended a couple of Twelve Step meetings on Saturday and pretty much rested my bones. Sunday morning came all too soon. I decided to go to a meeting on the south side. I had been under extreme pressure due to problems involving the church I had formerly attended – St. James. The female that had invited me there had been arrested for stalking me! I still felt uncomfortable and unsafe even though I was partially hiding out at HL's home in Fifth Ward.

I sat in the meeting listening to how people stay sober when I began to experience what felt like indigestion. I attempted to burp myself thinking that might do some good.

I got up and went to take a sip of water that did no good either! The burning began to increase in intensity. I decided to leave the meeting early and go to Mass at the charismatic Catholic church. The service was in full swing as I entered. I sat most uncomfortably experiencing sharper pains in my chest. I left the church and drove myself back to HL's home. Fortunately, his son was visiting from California that very weekend. I lay down on the living room sofa, and then it happened! I began to feel numbness and then tingling in my left arm and up my neck. I could swear an elephant was attempting to stand on my chest. I knew the warning signs from medical training years prior in the Air Force.

My voice was trembling as I called out for HL's son who came running immediately. I told him to dial 9-1-1; that I was having a heart attack. He called the number and within ten minutes Emergency Medical Technicians were hooking me up to a monitor and squirting Nitroglycerin under my tongue. I was headed for the Veteran's Medical Center post haste. The EMT observed my condition while on the way. As siren blared, he radioed in for permission to squirt another shot of "Nitro" under my tongue. We arrived and I was rushed into a waiting bed where a nurse hooked me up to more machines. Two physicians arrived and one asked if I was allergic to morphine. I answered, "No!" I was given a shot and the "elephant" began to leave my chest. The doctors took blood samples and listened intently to my heart. I asked what was going on and one of the two said, "Well, Mr. Keating, you're having a heart attack – coronary embolism [blood clot blocking an artery in the heart]." It never occurred to me that I might die! I just wanted the pain to go away, which it did with the IV shot of morphine. I was given a second "blast" of pain medication and I began to "nod off." Shades of my old opium habit were coming back to memory as my mind drifted into a twilight state. Oh blessed relief from the pain, at last!

Eventually, my condition was stabilized with blood thinners and more pain medication. I lay in the Intensive Cardiac Care Unit with a tube wrapped around my face pumping pure oxygen into my nostrils. I dozed off now and then due to the fact I was given an anti-anxiety medication to calm down my Type A Personality. Such people are wired for the fast lane only. And of course, such people usually get the same results that I was faced with, or worse! I was fortunate, indeed!

A nurse came in and asked if there was anyone she could contact and let them know where I was. I thought for a moment and decided to have her leave a message for my Creole Queen. A message was left for HL to let him know that I was still "sucking air." The rest of that Sunday, I lay quietly while doing my best to mentally speed up the recovery process that was a totally insane concept as if I had some sort of control over my present situation! That type of thinking was precisely what landed me in the hospital in the first place. The concept of shouting at a microwave oven to hurry up was not foreign to me at all! My life style had to change as I was to learn very soon! I had to learn to take time to "smell the flowers."

Dinner was the usual fare for hospitals, but in my case the menu had changed. Have you ever eaten a meal without any salt, sugar, fat, and baked to boot? Blaw! I did my best to be grateful for the grub, and say a special thank you to God for sparing my life. Just as I finished my short communication with God, my Creole Queen popped in the door with her son and one of his friends. She leaned over and kissed me tenderly in what I call a "double lip lock." Yes, we were "sucking serious face!" I had never been so glad to see anyone before. Her son whom I had a very good relationship leaned over and gave me a big hug. They both said how grateful to God they were that I was still "around." It felt so good to know that I was loved at that desperate moment. In spite of my self-centeredness, God was watching over me then and now.

My stay in the hospital was fairly brief – only two weeks. Rose came to visit almost every evening. We'd play Scrabble or just talk about the future. Yes, we were still considering marriage. We had discussed the fact that in the past she had not had the monetary where with all to pay for a divorce and find her deserting husband to serve him papers. I offered to pay for all of it, but she wouldn't hear of it. She said that she created the mess by rushing into marriage instead of listening to her Uncle and Auntie who did not approve of him. She mustered up the necessary funds to file the papers in Texas and have them served in Louisiana. This lady was serious about getting out from "under" now that she had the proper incentive – me! I lay there in the hospital not knowing whether I would be able to work in my high pressure position again, and yet, Rose wanted me anyway! Now, that's real love!

My stay in the hospital was to end on a Monday just before Thanksgiving weekend. I looked forward for the trip to Louisiana with the love of my life. Early on Thanksgiving Day we rose and headed east on the interstate highway with her son following in her car. She planned on staying for the entire week after the holiday to sign papers for her mother's residence in a rest home in Houma. As we cruised along at 75 mile per hour, Rose softly spoke words that I didn't fully comprehend. She said, "John, it's bad. Really bad! The family situation is falling apart. Maybe I didn't make myself clear before. I'm sorry to get you into this." She was having "second thoughts" about my visiting her parent's home, but it was too late. We were on our way. I said, "How bad could it be, Rose?" She paused and then began to emotionally dump what was really bothering her, "It's my sister. I told you she had a drug problem. Well, she brings men over to the family house for…you know." I retorted, "Okay, that's her choice. What's that got to do with you?" She said, "Nothing to do with me, but it's her little girl and my parents. My mother has dementia and father, well, he wears this thing on the 'front' of him." I said, "A Foley bag?" She answered with shame in her voice in the affirmative and then said, "Sometimes he forgets to empty it and it spills over. That's why I want to bring him back with me to Houston. He needs someone to look after him because my damned sister isn't. She's more interested in sucking on a crack pipe and 'other things'!" Rose was beside herself with rage. I asked her, "Well, whatever gives you peace of mind is all right with me, Sweetheart. If you say your father needs care with us in Houston, that's fine with me. I know you've had it rough." I paused for a moment and continued,

"Maybe, just maybe, I can ease some of that burden you've been carrying far too long." She reached over and placed her hand on my knee and said, "John that's why I love you so much. You're a good man! I'm so fortunate to have you as my friend." I calmly inquired, "You just called me your friend. What do you mean by that?" She replied, "It's a figure of speech, John. I meant nothing bad by it. You are my friend first of all and most of all." I said, "Yes dear." Yet, I was troubled by her reference. Was she ashamed of our relationship? Was she afraid of family rejection because of my color? Was she having second thoughts, suddenly? I wisely kept my mouth shut.

Our relationship became strained during the trip to the Delta. Something was troubling Rose, and I sensed that she needed "space." We had taken her father directly to the VA Hospital when we arrived back in Houston. The doctor gave him a fair bill of health. After we took him back to her apartment, Rose and I sat at the dining room table. She looked at me and said, "John, I'm so sorry! I know we looked at wedding rings and I said I wanted to marry you, but..." I cut her off in mid sentence and finished it for her, "You have to 'think'." That unique quirk of African American women came home to roost. It's just one of those things that simply has to be "worked out" within the heads of each sister when she's truly serious about a man. She has to have time alone to come to terms with the totality of the situation. She's weighing every possible issue in the relationship to make absolutely sure, it's going to work not just for her, but her "man." If she goes through the "thinking process" and she returns to the man, she is his for life and no man could ever ask for a more loyal friend. She'll die for him and think nothing of it! If she goes through the process and decides it's not a "go," The man will never hear from her again. She has to go through the process and it's hell on the man. He's stuck out feeling much like a little lost puppy until she's finished with the thinking process. It might seem cruel [on him], but actually it's a blessing. If he is wise, he'll "think" too! That's exactly what I decided to do. I wished Rose the very best and said, "Good bye." Why? I understood that I might never see her again!

I cried my eyes out for days secretly, but kept a smile on in public while she was "thinking."

She went out on a date with a man from a former relationship. She went dancing. She avoided meetings where I might be. Time dragged on and I continued to think also. I contacted Cherry. We met and I unloaded about how I felt about Rose's issue with her dark color. I felt that perhaps she was looking for approval because I was white. I discussed the fact that I couldn't "fix" Rose. I couldn't give her permission to accept herself just as she was. She had to find that on her own. I told Cherry that I thought that the issue could come up in the future and create more problems than I was not willing to face. Yes, I loved Rose dearly, but not at the cost of my own peace of mind. She had to find a solution to the color thing before we got married. Cherry concurred completely. Cherry said, "You're right, John. You can't make her happy. Happiness comes from self acceptance." I knew what I had to do – give myself time even if she came back with that all-important "yes." If I saw self-acceptance within her, then it would be a "go" for me as well as her. I didn't know how long that would be. That didn't matter. It had to be that way, and it hurt like hell!

Two months passed by and suddenly there she was at a meeting on the south side where I was continuing to attend. She came in all dressed up. She looked lovely as usual. I just couldn't find it in me at that moment to talk to her. I left the meeting early without saying a word to her. Eventually, we talked and I told her how I felt about her issue. She couldn't accept my diagnosis of her problem. She was in denial that her attraction to me might be based on "approval seeking." We parted company and, in time, she left Houston for Temple where she married the "other man" who was none other than "white." I was right after all, but damn it, I wished I wasn't! **Sometimes being right can feel totally wrong!**

Chapter Twelve
The Costs of Being

The recovery center where I worked on the south side of
Houston went through the process of "downsizing." I moved
to Pasadena to be near my Creole Queen. As time told, the
relationship ended and I lay stranded miles away from my new
job on the near north side in Fifth Ward. The commute was
horrendous in the mornings especially traveling toward Houston on
its busy freeway system. My new position put me in direct contact
with the man that had hired me at A Better Way, a few years
earlier. Mack was a tall, lanky brother who knew his stuff when it
came to counseling. We had bonded well. He used to call me his
"little brother in a different suit." I worked on the male unit and
got a reputation for being tough on clients. I'd ask them, "So, when
are you going to stop 'tricking' yourself?" Most black clients
hated me at first until they found out where I was "coming from" –
my frame of reference. I had learned Ebonics, which is commonly
called Black English. Some even asked me if I was black or white.
I had been asked the same thing when attending PV, years earlier
by a sister. My answer was always the same, "Should it matter?"
The response was always the same – silence and bowed head.

It was no big deal for me to share from my heart about never
meeting my biological father; having a biological mother turned
prostitute; being emotionally, physically and sexually abused,

facing the cold steel of jail house bars; having been in psyche wards for drug induced psychosis; and, being flat line dead at one point. Almost every client could identify with one or more parts of my life story. Brothers came to me privately and would lay it all out with their eyes filled to overflowing with tears. They knew that I was "on the real" and would "cut for them" if they were serious about sobriety. A black Counselor had once told me that my color would make it impossible for me to "reach" brothers and sisters. He was flat out wrong!

Work was going well and I continued to attend meetings on the south side of Houston. My counselor friends at the new facility kept telling me about this sister named Irma. She worked in house keeping at the facility. One Counselor even went so far as to say, "John, if I was you, I'd check her out! Tell you the truth, if I weren't already married, I'd 'hook up' in a heartbeat." My curiosity was peeking. The day came when she and two of her girl friends were sitting in what was called the "chicken coup." It got its name because of the wire mesh protecting persons from the elements while they smoked outside. Anyway, I sat down and they were cackling much like a bunch of hens. One of them looked over at me because I was smiling and trying not to laugh at their subject of conversation – male sexuality. She said, "Excuse me! What's so funny about what we're saying?" She had done that neck thing and I knew a scrap was brewing. I just couldn't resist. I jumped in the conversation much like diving into hot water headfirst. I held my own with this sister. Irma piped up and said, thinking that she could call my bluff, "White boy, you ain't had a woman until you've had a piece of me! Have you ever been with a sister before?" I sat there calmly in a moment of Spiritual weakness and inquired, "And you – sister – ain't had a man until he's vanilla!" She chuckled and retorted, "What you saying, big boy? You think you can handle a black woman?" I shrugged my shoulders and replied, "Small potatoes." The challenge was on – one strong black woman and one white boy who was keeping a secret or two.

She actually agreed to a date. I came by to pick her up at her apartment in the hood. She was a no show! Needless to say, that smarted a bit being that I had never been stood up for a date before in my entire life! I thought to myself, "This sister needs to be taught a lesson." The next Monday, at work, I encountered her in a hallway. I asked her point blank what went down on Saturday night. There was a long pause, and then she said something that made me respect her integrity. She looked at me and almost in a whisper said, "I was afraid." I came back with, "Of what?" She very quietly said, "I never dated a white man before." I had called her bluff. I must have had a stupefied look on my face as I mustered up the courage to ask, "Let's go out next Saturday night. We'll grab a bite to eat and catch a movie. How does that sound to you? And, I promise I won't bite you! I may nibble a little, but I won't bite. Okay?" With that said, she gave me her pager number and said she'd be ready at 6:30 PM sharp. She had courage, after all. Little did I realize just how much courage this sister had!

Sure enough, this time she was ready and dressed very well. She was in her mid-forties and of good figure. I learned that she was a widow. She had raised two boys in the hood. She had even gone to a technical school at night to study Hazardous Materials Handling! She lived alone in one of the roughest apartment complexes in Fifth Ward. She lived in "government subsidized housing." She was doing her best to "maintain." She was fiercely religious on Sundays being Baptist. She wouldn't miss services for anything. She had a thing for playing football pools when in season. She could bad-mouth you like a sailor when she had to. She sat silently in my car as we headed for the restaurant next to the theater I had picked out. It was in a "white area."

Irma evidently enjoyed the evening as I shook her hand good night at her doorstop. The date was over and I hadn't made one advance. I made it a point to be the perfect gentleman. I remembered what she had said about never dating a white man before. I was bound and determined to give her the right impression from the "get go." We began to see each other on a regular basis. We took trips to the beach, paddle boat riding, 3-D movies, shopping and just "kicking it." She had a wild sense of humor and loved to play practical jokes. We were starting to become an item around the work place. Males secretly asked me how the sex was, but to their disappointment, there was none. I truly respected Irma, and that confused her. She wondered if I was gay, or not? She was used to being "hit on" and using the "down low life style" to make ends meet. The hood does that even to the so-called "best of people."

We continued dating for over three months and then the relationship changed. Physical aspects evidenced themselves more out of curiosity from Irma's point of view than mine. Yes, Rose and I had been sexual. I might add that we both asked God to forgive us, also. Irma moved into my apartment while keeping her own for weekends. She remained fiercely religious on Sundays. I was not about to compete with her belief in God! I continued to attend Mass now and then. Problem was, that attendance had a slight sting because of memories of Rose. I wondered secretly if Irma and I would end up the same way. The "relationship thing" was a bogeyman! The scars of being the victim of racism where men simply disappeared out of survival sometimes ran deep in sisters. That competition thing between black males and females for jobs had set off a fierce gender war. Irma was no different in that respect. Even though I was clearly white, I was a male and "in the mix." She'd say to me, "The only thing white about you is your skin, bother!" She was serious!

Yes, our relationship had a few bumps and turns. We broke up a couple of times, but some how found ourselves back together. In time, I learned that Irma knew just about everybody in Fifth Ward – that's no exaggeration. She was a character, and she knew how to have a good time. We went out dancing together on Friday nights. She shared her issues with me including the fact that she had been a drug addict. Yes, she had been on "the corner." With two growing boys to feed, something had to give. Its called survival and I admire the fact that she didn't just surrender completely. She has a "get back up" spirit. That is what I respect most of all about Irma. In spite of Major Depression, unemployment, seeing relatives die and the list goes on, she just keeps on keeping on! In my humble opinion, you can't get any better than that!

Our relationship began to wane in the latter part of 2003. She seemed extremely unhappy. She had been placed on a new medication for her depression. She began to physically change because of the pills she took. They caused her to retain water. She began to loathe herself. She had taken pride in her excellent figure. Now she'd make comments about being a "fat girl." She ultimately said, "John, I'm not the one you should marry." Two days before Christmas, she went back to Fifth Ward. I took her "home" and only see her now and then. Culture plays cruel tricks on even the finest of intended behaviors. There are two lessons to be learned from Irma. Firstly, **you may take a person out of the hood, but it is most difficult to take the hood out of the person!** The second axiom is this: **Relationships never end, they just get different.** You may "end" seeing a person, but they are still there. Death my part peoples, but truth is, they live on in our hearts and memories. They are still with us until we finally pass over also.

My life began to unravel. I had lived the good life for a few years there. My apartment was plush. I had created an N-scale model railroad in the dinning room. I had everything a person would want including a home-entertainment center that others can only dream of. Christmas was miserable. I just felt like something was missing and I was out of place. I wrote a letter to the minister of St. James Church. I apologized even though I had done nothing wrong except hold bitterness for all that had gone down. It had been six years since I had walked into that church. I had no real desire to go back. I just wanted peace above all else.

February arrived and I chose to leave my apartment. I moved back to Houston. A friend helped me place my furniture in an abandoned warehouse for safekeeping. February 2nd was the date when I found myself back on the streets. I lived in the rear of that warehouse and applied for residence at an apartment complex for "homeless veterans." Life seemed that it couldn't get much worse. I sheepishly walked back into that church I left. I just wanted to worship, just like before. I had no desire to be a part of anything. I wanted nothing from them whatsoever.

The Bible says that there is a season for everything under heaven. That is so true. My stubbornness was gone. Unbeknownst to me, the Pastor had gone through some growing pains himself. The female that had invited me to the church in the first place had not learned her lessons. She placed herself in a situation where she was ultimately humiliated beyond belief. She goes through physical and emotional pain each day due to her own choice of rebelling against a Loving God. Her mind is completely "split" into two distinct personalities. She's the "church lady" sometimes and then flips to become the "prostitute" at others. Instead of dealing with her issues of sexual abuse as a young girl, she had tenaciously attempted to hide them. Such action has lead to not just the splitting of her personality, but she has abandoned the "little girl" that she should have taken care of deep within her psyche. She's losing her mind. She's becoming one more statistic of the shameful history of racism in America. I'm powerless to help her and I guess that's what hurts most of all. We used to be best friends. Now, I must protect myself from her lunacy.

Chapter Thirteen
The Problem and Its Origins

From the beginning of recorded history, man witnessed the opposing phenomena of light during the day and darkness at night. It's much easier to see during the day light hours, hence any person be it modern or caveman, would naturally feel safer to travel, cook or whatever the chore might be. During the night, those same persons will have a tinge of fear simply because they cannot see as well, or at all. The **association** of light being safe and darkness being a reason for fear was firmly established. The problem with this association is that is extends beyond just the phenomena of light and dark pertaining to the position of the earth relative to sun light.

The association is carried to the point to where persons who are lighter are perceived as being "safer" than those who are "darker." The idea that those whose complexion is lighter is glorified. Those with blue eyes and blonde hair are considered "superior." Some pseudo scientists have referred to these people as being the "ice people." Those being darker are considered inferior and have been called the "mud people." Such ideology is based on superstition, ignorance and paranoia. Yet, this ideology persists! A prime example is what the Nazis did to the Jews who were considered just another version of the "mud people." The association that light is related to rightness and darkness is evil is reflected not just in Nazi literature that is based on Social Darwinism, but is mentioned in the Bible itself. Even language reflects these pathetic attempts to mask our ignorance. Such words as "black mailed" connotes evil. Such phrases, as being the "black sheep of the family" is yet one more example of how darkness is evil. We carry this errant belief into the realm of skin color to the extreme.

It's no wonder that the issue of race becomes one of heated debate by many. The fact of the matter is that our associations do affect our perceptions of people, places and things. It is much like holding a microphone up to a speaker then turning on the amplifier all the way. Within a split second the phenomena of "feedback" can be heard screeching away! Until the amplifier is turned down, the phenomena will continue. Race is just like that microphone when it is brought up to most people. The screeching begins and becomes deafening until the idea of removing it as a "separating cause" is completed.

But, wait just a minute. How do we turn the amplifier down? We have become used to the screeching. We have become fatalistic about it. We accept the screeching as a way of life! We begin to deny that the screeching is going on. It dulls our sense of hearing and eventually deafens us all together to any other way of thinking. Some turn to surgery to cut the screeching out. Still others use hearing devices to better pick up "other sounds." One thing is for sure, in any case, pain will be experienced whether we learn to live with the screeching, go through surgery, or wear aids. New ideas must replace what we have been used to. That replacement will cause pain. It's unavoidable! The question then becomes which pain do we choose to experience? A lifestyle based on ignorance, superstition and paranoia or one filled with the risk of change, that's the choice!

It is the same with the issue of race. Some sort of outside phenomenon must be applied so that the issue that is literally damaging all of us is eliminated. But what effective aid might be applied so that we are no longer harmed as one people? **The first solution to the problem of race is acknowledgment of race as an issue worthy of our time and effort to eradicate.** We must have a goal, or idea, in mind before we even begin to tackle the problem. Some would call that goal a DREAM. We must muster up the willingness and courage to do something – anything – to reach the goal. If we don't want to change then the problem only becomes worse. There must be an honest desire to see and obtain the dream. There must be persistence, no matter how much resistance opposes our attainment of the goal. We must be willing to endure any hardship and pain to reach that blessed point of freedom for each and every person.

But wait a minute! Doesn't the issue of race affect our ability to reason? Doesn't it actually weaken our ability to reach any rational goal? The answer is yes, it most certainly does. It's like I mentioned in my story about how the mind that is working against us is the same organ we must use to work for us – a paradox! We focus on solutions to the issue instead of the problems that affect the issue. As we gain knowledge of the issue, we become more comfortable with the issue. We are more able to discuss the issue more rationally. We begin to accept the issue for what it really is. In time, it no longer becomes an issue, but instead, an asset to be valued. We begin to find the issue a desirable necessity in our lives. We become free from the negative effects of the issue. We begin to celebrate such an idea as this: **Variety is the spice of life!**

Let's define the issue and see if indeed it is "the issue" at all. Okay, let's say that race is the issue. Let's say that Charlie who is white doesn't like Tom who is black. Charlie sees Tom a specific way. Tom sees Charlie with a "reactionary view" of dislike. Both men are affected by what they perceive. They trust their perception because those same views have served them well in the past, or so they believe. After all, both have been taught that the other IS the problem. That is their perception – the other person causes my pain! It's his fault and that makes him my enemy! They fear each other that only leads to hatred of each other. More pain, kids!

Charlie and Tom are stuck in an environment filled with "feedback." They're going deaf ever so slowly. Eventually, they will reach a state of hopelessness where neither one can hear the other, even if they tried to communicate. They accept their condition as one of fate. That's the way it has always been, and that's the way it will always be. They both become comfortable with the status qou. They learn to exist with the problem flaring up now and then. They cannot sense that immanent danger is plaguing both of them. Those flare-ups, called riots, cost both Charlie and Tom something. Actually, it costs them much more than they realize. And yet, they continue to live with the feedback; accept their losses; and, expect everything to somehow magically work out. The flare-ups just keep happening, which both parties refuse to acknowledge, because they can't hear reason any more. Charlie and Tom seem hopeless, don't they?

Charlie and Tom have "expectations" of what the other might do at any time. With that state of mind brewing, suspicions of each other grow much like a virus – exponentially! They may speak to each other out of necessity whether it is at the grocery store, bank, work or shopping mall. They may do business like auto repairs, construction, carpet cleaning, yes even baby-sitting. It's "understood" that there are boundaries, each has "their place" in the "system." What Charlie and Tom do not understand is that both have been brainwashed by those who control the system to their advantage – being black as well as white. The system exists for the sole purpose of those on top to maintain their positions by any means necessary. They control eighty percent of the wealth in America. Their thesis is "divide and conquer." They use radio, television, movies, newspapers, magazines, books, government documentation and any other message they can muster to keep the "screeching" going on and deafen Charlie and Tom. They use "rap", "hip hop", "gangster noise", "love ballads", and yes, even "gospel" to deafen unsuspecting victims so they will tow the line! It isn't just a "white thing" here. The message is subtle and constant. If everyone stays in his or her places, the world will be all right! So, Charlie and Tom get a constant diet of racist dogma presented by none other than their own ethnic look-alikes – let's call them what they are COLLABORATORS. Our two victims believe their own because how could one of "their own" be so treacherous as to PREACH a dogma that dehumanizes, objectifies and eliminates both segments in one form or another?

TIME OUT: After World War Two, a Jewish Rabbi who was a Chaplain in the US Army visited one of the Nazi death camps. He stood at the edge of an open pit where the bloated yet emaciated bodies of over one thousand victims lay rotting away. A tear rolled down his cheek as he said to a Protestant Army Chaplain standing next to him, "The Germans hated themselves this much?" Lay the book down and just think about what that Rabbi asked. I'll be here when you get back.

Great, you're back! Did you get what he meant? Let me help you grasp his point just in case you haven't seen the light yet. We're back to Charlie and Tom. Charlie honestly believes that he is better than Tom by virtue of his "race." Charlie has behaviors that go along with his belief system. Now get this! Charlie won't be overt against Tom because down deep inside he has an uneasy feeling acting the way he does. Charlie would like to live in peace, but he's got a problem – let's call it **peer pressure**. If Charlie should get too close to Tom for any reason, Charlie knows it will cost him something. His next-door neighbor my snub him at the grocery store. He may even lose a job, if he dares to do the right thing as some call it. He becomes a "cultural misfit." He understands that is the lowest form of life on earth. So, Charlie goes along with the status quo because he sees Tom as the problem. He has rationalized, intellectualized and justified his position because if he doesn't, he's going to feel pain from his peers. We're back to "that's the way it has always been." That's a safe position to take whether you are white or **black**!

Now, this is where things get real interesting. Charlie rings his hands when the subject of race comes up. He actually begins to sweat. Why? Because down deep he feels his world view might be a "little bit wrong." He might even be willing to take a "little" of the blame for all the pain. But, the fact remains that Charlie is armed with excuses because he's been brainwashed – just like Tom. Charlie exclaims in exasperation, "If they could be just like me, everything would be all right [more acceptable]!" Charlie has even said, "Why, some of my best friends are…" He's even given money so black kids can go to college to make himself feel better. Truth is, some black folks know this and "play" on Charlie's guilt. It solves nothing! Charlie is confronted on the jokes he's said that presumably means nothing. Eventually, he demands that the subject of race be changed to something less flammable. Problem is that Charlie is the subject here, not race!

But wait just a minute here, there are two players in this dangerous game leading to flare-ups. Tom, who seems absolutely innocent, doesn't realize that he is contributing to the perpetuation of the problem also. Tom, to be sure, has a number of valid reasons as to why he should avoid Charlie by any legal means necessary. He feels fear, loathing, rage and deep hurt whenever he comes near Charlie. At times, the best thing Tom can do is lock himself up in a closet and just scream his head off! He has to let the pain out some time or be considered certifiably insane. He leaves his house wearing his "Mr. Charlie face." He encounters Charlie, but Charlie doesn't have a clue as to what's behind the smile and friendly greeting he gets from Tom. Charlie doesn't perceive Tom's pain because Tom has been taught from infancy, "Smile for Mr. Charlie. It's the safe thing to do!" But, what if Tom decided to at least stop smiling. He wouldn't have to say anything to Charlie about why he's not smiling. Hummmmm? What do you think might happen? To this point, Tom is showing Charlie what he thinks he's supposed to exhibit for Charlie's benefit and his own survival. At least, that's what the "brainwashers" have taught us – both white and **black**!

Hey Tom, guess what? You are not doing Charlie or yourself a favor by keeping the "face" on. Let me put it this way, "You be the problem too!" You're perpetuating the ignorance, superstition and paranoia that both you and Charlie share equally! The truth is, if Charlie really knew how you felt, it would scare the living hell out of him. But then again, the way things are simply amplify the real problem – our perceptions of each other! Let's take a look at Charlie and Tom at the annual Christmas party. Let's say they work for the same company. Let's say they must interact on a daily basis. We're entering the realm of Reality Therapy, kids. Let's say both Tom and Charlie have had a little too much "joy juice." Let's say that Charlie's feeling depressed about Christmas. He approaches Tom. He begins to emotionally dump his crap. Tom doesn't want to hear Charlie's crap, he's got enough of his own. He tries to avoid Charlie. Charlie wonders why. Eventually, Tom tries to leave the party because he's been "conditioned" to not air dirty laundry in public, especially if Mr. Charlie is around. Charlie – out of guilt – tries to understand why Tom is avoiding him. He brings up the word – oh God, not race! Tom immediately goes on the defensive and tries everything to end the subject. After all, everything is Charlie's fault anyway. Tom leaves. Charlie is left standing there full of frustration because he doesn't know Tom at all! Why Tom? Why doesn't Charlie know the real you? It goes back to that "conditioning" thing. Both sides believe the crap that has been taught them. Nothing is accomplished until somebody is willing to take a risk. Yes, it's painful. But my God, isn't your present situation just as painful? What could Tom have done differently? How about Tom letting Charlie know that the subject of race makes him feel unsafe, fearful and full of anger? Most Charlies feel the same thing, but from a different viewpoint. Tom, if you want to change Charlie, stop avoiding him. If, per chance, he should bring up the race thing. There are ways of showing him that you are a "real person" with the same wants and needs as his. We're going there, kids!

First of all, when you are hurt – SAY SO! But, you don't have to "go off" on others. Let me give you a real life example of what I mean. I sat facing the President of the New National Black Political Party [not the real name]. He was saying what he "thought and believed" I needed to hear. He "thought" he was talking to Mr. Charlie. He went on about white oppression and injustice. I nodded my head in agreement. After all, he was absolutely correct. All that DOES exist. When he was done, he sat back with this air of "whipping whitey's ass." I leaned forward and very kindly said this, "Mr. X, please take good care of yourself physically, emotionally and especially, Spiritually. I want you to be around a good, long time. You want to know why?" There was a long pause and then I blew his mind. I said almost at the point of tears, "Because I love you, just the way you are, Mr. X." He just sat there studying my face. He saw that I was "for real." There was not a thing he could say! He very quietly got up and walked away continuing to keep an eye on me as he left. I haven't personally seen hide, nor hair of him since. I have seen him on television mouthing what he honestly believes everyone needs to hear. To a point, he's absolutely correct. I DO believe that racism does exist. I DO believe that everyone is being hurt by it. EVERYONE! I DO know that there are those – both white and black – who want things to stay just the way they are. They're making money off the "system." But, I also believe that I don't have to be a player in the game either.

Now X has a certain amount of power behind him. He could have had me killed. But, that's not what has happened. Check this out! When you choose to show love to others, one of three reactions will come at you. Others will either want to kill you; run from you [because they think you're nuts]; or, they are going to love you back! Now those are very good odds, indeed! Hey, that's better than playing lottery! Two-thirds chances of getting what you want! Either being left alone, or being loved! How you present yourself keeps the first odd of happening, usually. Even if it should come to that, you will be more free than you've ever experienced living on this old Earth! God isn't going to keep you out of Heaven for being a racist or bigot because you're not one! The ball is in the other person's court, if you please. You're free! No, it couldn't be that simple. Here's what each individual can do to get free.

Charlie has to come to terms with his part in the problem, just like Tom. Charlie has to look at the history for what it is and acknowledge it's evil. To be sure, that view will be uncomfortable at first. Charlie has to be willing to admit that his ancestors and yes, he had/has a part in it. Charlie has to be willing to go the "extra mile" to right the wrongs, one person at a time. Charlie has to "rub shoulders" with all the Toms he encounters even when they want to "whip his ass" verbally or otherwise. Charlie has to recognize that he isn't as superior as he thinks. So much for **white privilege**. Most importantly, Charlie must smash the amplifier all to hell. We are what we eat! Whether what we consume is physical food or emotional messages from media and others, it comes back out eventually. The Bible says it another way, "As a man thinks, so is he." IF I'm "feeding" on garbage that's exactly what I will become! Some of you readers are thinking, "But, you don't understand! Hell, you ain't black! You haven't felt the sting of being called a nigger. Who do you think you are, white boy?" My answer is this, "And, who do you think you are? Haven't you had enough pain yet? It ain't going away until you do something about it, TOM!" Whether you're Charlie or Tom, you have to decide if you want to die with the cancer in you, or go for surgery. Ouch! Yes, it's going to hurt, but are there any rewards for actually "doing the right thing?" You bet there are! You see, I sleep well at night. Why? Because I know beyond a shadow of a doubt I have not intentionally hurt another human being for any reason at any time. Now, that's a good thing! My blood pressure is lower, my heart beat is slower, my nerves aren't on edge, my digestion works better, my life actually has been extended! I'm free! But, first we have to get down to how we get that freedom. Prepare yourselves for surgery, kids!

Chapter Fourteen
What We Have Done To Each Other

Charlie, don't put the book down here! You too, Tom! This is where you two get free.

Charlie, Tom's ancestors were captured by tribal rivals back in Africa for a few trinkets. Their ancestors were taken in chains and packed like sardines in the holds of slave ships. At least half the "cargo" died on the way to the Americas. They were sold into slavery and became the "property" of white folks primarily. Now Tom, some of your folks did own other black slaves. That's a fact! Whether the owner was white or "light, bright and almost white", they did the same brutal things. There were beatings, whippings, raping, mutilations, lynching, and the list of madness goes one. White and black lived in fear. Black folk lived in fear of being further brutalized. White folk lived with the very real possibility of violent reaction from blacks. Everybody suffered to one degree or another. EVERYBODY! And this social structure exists to this day! That's where acknowledgment is so important. We must recognize not just the past, but the very real present. We must acknowledge the fact that EVERYBODY has a part in the perpetuation of racism and reactionary bigotry. Both do exist, and both "feed" on each other! That's where the "feedback" exists. That eight-tenths of one percent of the US population knows this all to well. Remember, what WE feed on is what WE become. That .8% seems to control our "diet." Or, does it?

Charlie, you know the past and can recite, almost verbatim, textbooks about slavery, "Jim Crow" segregation, discrimination and all the rest. You feel just a little bit guilty, don't you? Hey, Tom! Stop gloating, because you're contributing to the problem also. Remember the Christmas party? Neither one of the players were honest! They managed to pour more salt in the wounds of the other. At this point Tom is saying, "Say what? Mr. Charlie ain't got no wounds, it's all my people!" Not so! Let's take a look at just one ethnic group who came to America, shall we Tom?

Way back in the late 1840s, there was a man-made famine in Ireland. The common potato that the population depended on for survival had a virus introduced by the British. Before the famine ended, over three million Irish starved to death. Another three million escaped aboard ships primarily for the United States. Many of those ships arrived in New York where the Irish were greeted with signs that read: NO DOGS OR IRISH ALLOWED! These fiercely religious immigrants died by the thousands in coal mines, laying rails, being raped in rich folks homes, coming down with diseases and just plain being starved in America. But wait there's more!

Many ships arrived in New Orleans. Wealthy white plantation owners greeted the immigrants at the docks. The immigrants were offered a shiny, new nickel to come "do some work" on the plantations. So, they followed the owners "home." They were given shovels, hoes, pitchforks and wheelbarrows. They were taken out to the swamps to dig ditches to drain the land so the plantation owners could have more land to grow cotton, sugar cane, sweet potatoes and other crops. The work was hard, filthy and dangerous. Over 80% of the Irish labor died of snakebites and alligators feeding. Some Irish escaped to a place called Texas. Most didn't make it. Native Americans killed them!

Now here's the kicker in this tale. The white plantation owners would rather kill thousands of Irish than use their black slaves. Why? Slaves were paid for in gold, not paper money! They were worth too much to be used for such dangerous and menial labor such as draining swamps. From the point of view of the Irish, those "darkies" had it good! There was truth to their point of view. The Irish were viewed as "subhuman" and dangerous because they were Papists (Roman Catholics)! Hey Tom, ask any Irishman what saved their ancestors from complete genocide in America, and you'll get the same answer. It was their collective belief in the Catholic Church. They would rather die than give up that Spiritual security. And Tom, did you know that the Irish weren't even considered "white" until the mid-nineteen twenties? Yes, I know your argument. They're white today, while I'm still being discriminated against. Okay, let's go with your argument for a moment.

Yes, it's true those Irish somehow became "magically" white. They did something that YOU haven't learned to do yet! They stuck together, they supported each other, especially when they went to church. They carried that "unity" back to the streets that they learned in church. But there's one thing you might have not considered. The reason Rev. Dr. Martin Luther King, Jr. was able to advance the Civil Rights Movement was because two Irishmen hadn't forgotten THEIR HISTORY – John and Robert Kennedy. They knew what it was to be called the "Niggers of Northwest Europe." They knew that their own had been sold into slavery by the British to Russians, Germans and points west, namely to the West Indies. Irish males were beaten to make them "breed" with black slave women to create a "lighter product" to be sold in America! Most Irish slave males refused to collaborate and were killed. It was their unshakable religious belief that kept them halfway sane and alive, but not always. Many did die because they refused to "breed." And those two Irish boys from Boston attempted to "pass on" the freedom they had earned. It cost them their lives! Now Tom, that's the truth, like it or not. You and yours have never been in the problem by yourself. Did you know that one out of four persons who were murdered during the Civil Rights Movement were white, as you call them? They could have watched television at home, but they didn't. They knew the risks and were willing to "give it all" because they believed, and still do believe, you're worth it! Charlie and Tom, you two need to come to terms with one thing: Like it or not, we're on this old Earth together. Whether we like it or not, that's the way it really is. So, why not make the best of it and at least "get along." Of course, my meaning of getting long isn't accepting the status quo. Not by a long shot!

There was a Black Panther from the sixties who said it best: "If you're not part of the solution, then you're a part of the problem." No truer words have ever been spoken. If I see someone, regardless of whatever who is being abused in any way for any reason and I say nothing, then I am as guilty as the perpetrator his or her self. I dare not attempt to "justify" my silence by saying, "Well, whitey got his come upping. He deserved it when one of my 'bothers' did whatever to 'get back'." OR, when I watch television and see where yet another black church has been burned to the ground and I don't do anything, I might as well have been there with the torch myself! There will come a time when I must give an account for not just what I did on Earth, but what I didn't do. There's this scripture that says, "How can you say you love God Whom you have not seen when you hate your brother whom you have?" But, what is hatred?

Hatred is not just overt acts of brutality or violence against another person. Oh no! All actions begin with thoughts. Remember earlier when I wrote that "as a man thinks, so is he." Somewhere along my walk in life, I must acknowledge my guilt, I must admit or confess my guilt and I must change my thinking and actions. That takes Spiritual surgery! I cannot get "clean" by myself. I must have a Higher Power Whom I surrender to. That Power must be everything or nothing. There's no middle ground. If I call myself by Christ Jesus' precious name then I must be OBEDIENT to His command. Whether I like it or not is beside the point. But, here's the good part. God always gives me what I wanted all along. He gives me the desires of my heart. The reason I drank and used drugs is because I didn't like the way I felt about myself. How could I possibly love anyone when I hated myself. We all use some kind of drug so we don't have to look at ourselves. Your drug my be food, clothing, cars, work, sex and the list goes on. It's not just alcohol or other chemicals. Not by a long shot. If I'm not following Christ's two simple rules for living then

I'm falling short of His goal for my life. Those two rules are these: Love the Lord God with all of your heart, soul and might; and the second is equal to it, Love your neighbor as you love your self.

You see, I'm not that "religious". Yes, I attend Mass from time to time. I even visit other churches. A statement was made years ago that, unfortunately, remains true today – the most segregated time of the week is eleven AM on Sunday! That's why I take as a grain of salt all those flowery words I hear on radio and see on television coming from the mouths of ministers and priests about love. That word is so abused that few persons really understand what it means today. The best description of love I've ever heard came from a Roman Catholic Priest who said, "Love, real love, is accepting people exactly where they are; respecting their views whether I agree or not; and allowing them to find their own way – right or wrong." I dare not play God and "preach" at anyone. I must take stock of what's in my inventory and get rid of the bad merchandise. I do this on a daily basis and eventually I'm free of what ails me! Not you, just me! That's all I can change. That comes through surgery on my heart. The bad stuff has got to go, if I am to consider myself a "true believer" in my God.

What changed my life and kept me from being a flaming racist all of my life was the love of one semi literate common law wife of a black sharecropper. She loved me unreservedly. She held me in her arms, rocked me back and forth, sang gospel to me and allowed me to fall asleep in her lap. She had every reason to hate the hell out of white people, but she loved a little, troubled white boy – ME! She had planted a seed that when watered by others later on, changed my heart and lifestyle to the point that I would never be the same. As that brother in the SBC church said, "I knew too much!" Yes, the surgery was uncomfortable in the beginning. I didn't understand what in God's name was going on, but I heard about this "dreamer" who said that we, as a people, will make it to the Promised Land. We can stand hand in hand and sing that old Negro spiritual that says "Free at last, free at last. Thank God Almighty, we're free at last!"

Here's the awful truth. We are all sick unto death with this race crap. We got it from our ancestors way back when they came out of caves. They associated light and dark to safety and danger. They carried that ignorance, superstition and paranoia right into the present. I can only speak for myself when I write, it was the love of just one person who changed my heart. Charlie and Tom, are you listening?

When I attended Prairie View A & M University, I encountered a sister who really "opened up" to me. She sat with tears rolling down her cheeks relating how her own family called her an "uppity nigger want to be" because she desired to get a higher education. They said, "Next thing you know, you'll be 'hooking up' with a white man and having little 'zebras'. You'll be too good for us!" Now, that's her own family! She sat there telling me "what time it is." I helped her study for exams. I had to because, you see Charlie and Tom, I chose not to be part of the problem anymore. I wanted freedom that much. That's why when I graduated I received applause from my peers. Of course, my peers had changed. They weren't just white anymore. They had become the colors of a whole new rainbow. I wouldn't have it any other way, really!

Tom and Charlie, there is a price to be paid for what I have. The first thing I had to admit was that I just might be wrong about everything. Secondly, I had to recognize that I was the problem and desperately needed help. Thirdly, I had to ask for aid from a Power greater than myself. My Higher Power is a man named David bar Yeshua Hamashiac Emmanuel – Jesus, from the lineage of David, Prince of Peace, God with Us. I had to accept and follow His teachings without reservation and despite my feelings. I had to " eat some humble pie" and open my closed mind. In doing so, slowly and surely the "old things passed away and all things became new." I don't talk about eradicating racism, or reactionary bigotry, I can't do anything about that. But, I can pray for wisdom, patience, tolerance and a whole lot of love for me [by me] and to and for others. I can simply "walk what I talk" on a daily basis. That's all I can do! If others don't like what I choose to live, that has to be their problem. Remember, the odds are with you, if you choose to change. If someone chooses to hate, then welcome to the world of physical and mental stress that equals eventual illness. And, welcome to the heartbreak of Spiritual darkness where separation from a Loving God is not a possibility, but fact! The other two odds are fantastic. Those who choose to hate me will either run like hell, or they're going to love me back. In either case, I'm one happy camper.

There is so much more that I could write, but I think my point has been made – positive change is possible through honest effort and the aid of a Loving God. Now, here's a message to all those middle-aged white males out there who were raised by Mammies as I was – go for it! Find that lady and thank her for what she gave you. It was more than you may realize until you begin the journey. She gave you a world view that, if nurtured, will offer you opportunities for adventure that you never dreamed possible. Yes, some black folks will think you're absolutely crazy. Some may call you a "honky." Family members may view you with suspicion when you begin your search – especially jealous wives! They will not understand, believe me! You may be accused of "looking for something different [sexually speaking]." Truth is, you just might find it! But keep in mind, your intentions must be pure. The reason I began my search was to express gratitude and to give back what was so freely given to me. And yes, I got back more than I ever dreamed imaginable. I wouldn't change a thing. I'm very rich because I have not just one culture, but three to derive strength and wisdom from – Western European, Asian and African!

So, I close with thoughts from my heart to yours regardless of your age, gender, religion, ethnicity, lifestyle or nationality. Life is to be lived to the fullest. It is not for the timid. It's like swimming in a pool – you're either going to sink or learn to move on. Love is not a feeling; it is an action instigated by thoughts from your mind. I can say anything, but until I go with what is right – it's much like "tinkling cymbals and sounding brass." I can believe anything, but to know something, I must experience it for myself. How I see anything is based on the collective consciousness of all that makes me what I am – past and present. Just because my family, clergy, other authorities say something might be right, doesn't make it so. I have to be willing to stick my neck out there and experience for myself whether a thing is true or not. I dare not depend on the knowledge of others, they may be self-doomed to everlasting ignorance in spite of educational attainment. I dare not believe that cause and effect are merely the product of irrational unseen forces, but rather there is a plan where I do fit in for a greater purpose that a Loving God has pre-ordained. I dare not depend upon my feelings based in what I cannot see, feel or experience. In other words, my ignorance, superstition and paranoia must go the way of the dinosaurs. Then and only then can I be truly free. I'll leave you with this scientific fact. Everyone on planet Earth is at the very least one-fiftieth cousin. When I say I hate someone else for any reason, I'm hating my own family, hence myself! Remember the rabbi?

Charlie and Tom, I hope and pray you have learned something about being you. If you can see each other as being "precious gifts" [to each other] then you can have what God has given me. Variety really is the spice of life. Just think how dull life would be if all of us looked, acted and believed exactly the same. I can appreciate classical music, rock and roll, gospel, rhythm and blues, jazz, country, even polka. Yes, I do have my preferences, but I choose not to limit myself. There's a big, beautiful world outside my window and I don't want to miss any of it. And, by the way, skin color doesn't rub off. If that were true then I'd be the strangest thing you'd ever see – red, yellow, black, brown and white. Been there and done that around the world, and I'm still ME, a very special short, four-eyed, white boy who has been given so much starting with love from Eula. Wherever you are "sister-girl" I love you and always will. You are my Spiritual mother!

Charlie and Tom, may God bless you and keep you, and may He give you His peace forever and always. Until we meet, just keep smiling. It looks good on your face!

Chapter Fifteen
Breaking You Off A Piece

One thing that you will not see in this book is a bunch of boring statistical data on the subject of racial issues. You received a small taste earlier about the female victims of sexual abuse. That's enough! However, lets take a look at the ramifications of the Civil Rights Movement from the point of view of the person on the street. Prior to 1960, a minimum of 65% of white males living primarily in the southeastern states of America were raised by African American females. Now, think about that for a second. The total number of males raised in such circumstances may never be known. It would be logical to assume that there are literally thousands upon thousands that have spread across the United States! So, what on earth does that mean? It's simple. Each one of those encounters represents a Spiritual seed that was planted in their hearts and minds. There ages range from the early forties up to the eighties. The caregivers – Mammies – would naturally be older, if indeed they are still with us at all. So, time is running out!

But, why the urgency in this particular matter? Well, let me break you off a piece of information about white males that I have personally spoken with. They range in age from their mid-forties through their early sixties. As I spoke with each man privately, specific questions were asked just to see how deep the imprinting might be where each male feels a significant bonding, or affection, for their former baby-sitters in some cases. You read about the fellow who wanted to set up the college fund for African American students naming such an endeavor after his former caregiver. Remember? He couldn't find her, and Lord knows, he looked far and wide.

I asked each gentleman if indeed he did have at least six months contact with his black female caregiver. Most said that they had more time than that. Some had years of contact. I asked each man if he had stayed in contact with his former sitter. One had maintained contact over the years. He was about fifty. The next question was deliberately aimed at their emotional ties to these ladies. I simply asked each one how they felt at the present time about their caregiver. To a man, they all stated that they felt deep affection and respect for her, the word love came up several times. I guessed here when I say that well over half gave that verbal cue of love. They volunteered the word.

I then asked them if they had experienced contact with African American culture. Again, over half said that they had regular contact with persons of color without incident. I asked them how they felt about African Americans in general. To a man, they all said that they admired the culture to one degree or another. Most listened at least half the time to so-called black radio stations. Then came the questions that really told just how deep the imprinting, or identification, with black people was. I asked each man privately if he had experienced intimate relations with ladies of color whether legitimate or illegal. Almost three-fourths said that they had been with ladies of color. I asked if such relations were legitimate – above board on regular dates. About a three of these men said that they indeed had experienced at least one date with a "sister." Only three of the males experienced relations through prostitution. I had asked nineteen men these non-scientific questions just to get an idea of how these wonderful ladies had affected these white males. Now, keep in mind, that this was not a true statistical analysis of the topic of such relationships. But, there still remains a significant share of males who remember with great fondness their African American caregivers from years prior. So, why would this be so important?

Okay, think about it for a minute. What if even one-third of the males figured in to those statistics prior to 1960 decided to find their former caregivers just to say thank you? Can you imagine the impact on black and white societies? Now here's the view of these men searching across America making calls, writing letters, and yes, even sending money to aid their former Mammies. Imagine these males coming to terms with racism as I did. Imagine how many men who were considered the "enemy" now could be considered allies for life to support African American causes, as I do! Oh, but there's a hitch in this scenario.

I was discussing the writing of this book with a fellow case manager. She is an early forties sister who made a very astute observation. She said, "Yes, that would be beautiful to see these men make amends and peace. But John, I can see a problem. Want to know what I see?" I nodded. She asked, "Who would be most vehemently against your book and its effects?" I shrugged my shoulders as she continued, "White women!"

I retorted, "Say what?" She said laughingly, "Yes, white women. When they find out that their husbands are searching for any black woman, sparks are going to fly! All hell is going to break loose." She paused and continued, "You may only reach active and former Klan members who would find themselves irresistibly drawn to the search. But, your real problem will come from jealous white women who simply will not understand that Spiritual bond between these white men and their former black caregivers. They are going to be mad as hell! Especially, if these husbands find themselves talking to attractive sisters who may be the younger relatives of these caregivers. I'm telling you John, they are going to eat you alive for starting this thing! I hope you live!" I chuckled, but then remembered some of the things I learned in my dialogue about racism. It doesn't make sense – it's irrational!

So, you gentlemen who have read the book thus far, be forewarned. If you are still married, there may be moments of tenseness from your mates. But, I guarantee that if you find your caregiver, it will be worth the time and expense to relive those memories with her. After all, we – as white males – do owe a debt for all that they gave. Permit me to explain.

Consider that she probably came some distance to arrive early in the morning to make sure that you were fed, washed, clothed and ready for school. She picked up after your messy selves. She did your laundry, cleaned the house, changed the linens and may very well have done the windows. Everything was perfect daily. She may very well have been there to at least fix your Sunday dinner. She received very little for her salary. I dare you to check on it for yourselves. And think of this, did you ever think about the children she may have had at her home who didn't get all that love and care, you received? Albeit, for a price! Yes, she made sacrifices way beyond what you ever imagined because they usually cared well for their little charges. Why? Not just to get a paycheck, hell no! Whether you recognized it or not, that "bonding" went both ways! Remember that Eula remembered me. She went above and beyond because there was a Spirituality about her that demanded the very best. I'd go so far as to say that she prayed for you when you didn't even know it. Ain't no pay for that! Yes, you got a great life growing up, if you had a Mammy. And of course, they shouted at you when you needed because they cared for you. They wanted you to grow up to be good citizens. Why? Because it was in their culture's interest to create as many allies against the system as possible. You might even consider them Trojan Horses, in a way! These ladies of color listened to everything. They talked too, but not around white folk. Imagine the conversations your caregiver may have had about you! Were you a good little white boy, or not? There's only one way to find out. Start searching!

Where do I begin such a search? The last place you saw her! It's kind of like losing your wallet, or keys, they are always in the last place you left them! Always! Okay, so she's not there. Unless she was a spinster, she's got relatives somewhere. Do you remember her name? Check with folks with the same name in that area. You may get lucky, then again you may get cold shoulders. Be very specific as to why you are on your search. Be totally honest, blacks folks can tell for sure! You see, they have to be intuitive considering what they've been up against for centuries. Remember this, whomever you contact doesn't know you from a hill of beans. You ARE going to look like a fool! Trust me on that. The vast majority of black folk WILL be polite. That goes back to the "Mr. Charlie Syndrome", especially the elderly African Americans you wish to speak with who may very well know exactly what you want to know. You won't know it though. They are going to smile and wish you good luck. You get nothing but frustration and exasperation.

Hey, wait a minute? That's what I get for my troubles? Let me break you off another piece of information. You, white boy, are used to getting what you want, when you want it. Chances are the only time you've had to wait for anything is when you were in the military; "Hurry up and wait!" Black folks have been waiting their entire lives for just a little piece of the pie. Some of the old timers may still be waiting for their mules. They gave up on the forty! That's a wry sense of humor for the black folks that are reading this. So, get used to running in circles. When they KNOW you are for real and aren't trying to "shine" them, you'll get the reward of your life. Trust me! I'm speaking from personal experience. You will be tested. You dare not forget their history. YOU are the enemy until you can prove beyond a shadow of a doubt that your motives are absolutely right on! Oh yes, and you might want to get used to the taste of "humble pie." They are not intending to humiliate you, they just want to know your "reality state." What do I mean by that? Not only will they probably think you're a fool, but certifiably insane. When you consider that the majority of white folks who venture into the hood are looking for drugs or sex, YOU coming in looking for your Mammy will be a hoot! Keep this in mind, after you discuss your search with just one black person, I guarantee EVERYBODY will know. But, you won't! I strongly suggest two things before you even think about starting your search.

Firstly, I'd seek therapy from a Counselor, Psychotherapist, Minister or Priest. You must make sure that your motives are absolutely correct. Remember, you are not just looking for a person – this is a Spiritual quest. You are going to find out more about yourself than you ever dreamed possible. And, I guarantee you will NEVER be the same. Remember that gentleman from the SBC church? He said I knew too much and there was no turning back for me. He was right on! You CAN expect tears, if you're lucky. The chickens are going to come home to roost, if you please. But, if you stick with it and prove yourself worthy, in time, you will be rewarded!

Secondly, I'd just take a drive through "that part of town" as you have always called it. OPEN YOUR EYES! Don't say anything to anyone, just drive quietly. Examine what you are feeling. Is it fear? That's telling you that you are not ready for the search. Speaking from my own experience, I have driven in the Bottoms of Fifth Ward at 3:00 AM with a brother hunched down and wearing "colors." He trusted me that much! I sat and watched folks "deal" right in front of me. They knew that I know it ain't none of my business. I've sat in the late evening listening to a quartet known for their gospel singing in the back of a store just for pleasure, and it was as if I were not there. So, how did I get to that point? I got to know just one person who let it be known that "He be good people, let him be." That, Sir, will take you time and a very open attitude. The slightest hesitation will get you screwed, maybe even killed. Intuition is everything!

One other thing and then I have a short message for my African American brothers and sisters. When you get to that point as you find yourself on "their turf," remember this – YOU AIN'T SQUAT! They don't have to give you a damn thing – it's the other way around. YOU OWE! That's where the humble pie comes in, make no mistake about it! I wish you all the best in your search. God bless you!

And now to all those beautiful folks who have made my life so very rich and sweet, I'm asking you from the bottom of my heart to cut these "white boys" some slack – PLEASE! Let's take a look at why it may be to your benefit, shall we?

Remember the businessman who wanted so desperately to find his caregiver to name the college fund after her? He isn't alone! Remember, Eula needed a few "dead presidents" to fix her hair. She got what she wanted as soon as the postman could carry it! Even though I was in school and couldn't afford much of anything, Eula got priority. I'm not saying that to show how good I am, but rather, to illustrate how important she was and will always be to me! Remember, that most of these searchers will be middle aged and middle class for the most part. They have money. Maybe not enough to burn, but most will be generous to a fault. Why? Oh come on now, you already know the answer — they guilty as hell! But, they also have precious memories of a lady who literally raised them, perhaps nursed them from their breasts. These men haven't forgotten those facts. It's like that seed that Eula planted in my heart 42 years before. Someone came along and "triggered" the water sprinkler that caused all the rest to happen. So, please keep in mind, they mean no harm and may very well be a blessing to a few of these ladies who might be "down on their luck."

I'm going to close with this. Perhaps, you folks of color may now understand why I was asked at places if I was black or white, as well as a few other places. And, why my former boss at the treatment center said, "He's a brother with a different kind of suit on." I guess I am, and I'm okay with that! Some of you may be concerned because I let out some of your "secrets." All I can say is this. Do you know "what time it is?"

A long, long time ago when you all were divided between those in the "patch" and those in the "house" most of those within sacrificed more than they would ever wish to be known to save the folks in the field, especially their men folk. Truth is the color barrier was smashed all to hell when the first Trojan Horse entered the "castle" of the master. Those red necked, pot bellied good old boys had no idea what was going on. If, per chance they did, they kept it to themselves. Truth is, those boys thought enough of some of you to trust their most precious belongings to you – their wives and children. They had opened the door way back when. And, they still are in some cases today. My parents opened the door all the way in the fifties when that sort of thing just wasn't done. If they hadn't, this book would have never been written! This short, four-eyed white boy wouldn't be saying the following: There are some of us who love all of you more than you will ever know. It's not out of guilt. To the contrary, it's out of real appreciation for all that you have given me. I am rich indeed! And, I've learned to have a really good time – party hardy, get down and boogie! So, again I ask you to please open the door just a little bit, it might prove to be the best decision you've ever made.

Epilogue
June, 2005

Well folks, this where we round things up and I say a few parting words. Please bare with me, I'm shedding a few tears. To all those people mentioned in the book, thanks for your lessons. To those who are reading it now, hey kids, let's "get along", shall we? It is possible to change, maybe not the whole world, or even all of America; but, one person at a time as we reach out and touch with our hearts anyone and everyone who chooses to listen and learn from the past. It simply doesn't have to be the way it has always been. That's were the hope is. Come on board this train bound for Glory Land. Oh what a ride it has been, and continues to be for one short, four-eyed white boy who was loved at the right time for all the right reasons by a black angel named Eula.

The "Players"

That Native American woman was never heard from again. I do hope she got the help she so desperately needed.

Tom and the mule found peace years ago. God bless him, and the mule too!

The Hawaiian Princess became a Psychologist. Hope she found the right man.

The California Girl went back home to San Diego. She had kids and then ended up in divorce court.

"Linda" probably retired with her taxi service and maybe, if she were lucky, a man to take care of her in her aging years. But, that's highly unlikely in her culture.

That Sunday school teacher retired from his occupation and ultimately went home to meet his Maker.

The female student at the Bible College who was expelled continued to "use." I can only pray that she found peace from her troubled life.

Miss Geraldine Dollar became the number three "higher up" in the entire Mental Health and Mental Retardation Authority of Houston, Harris County. You go girl!

My ex-wife is nearing retirement and has been "co-dependent free" for years now. She's in my daily prayers.

Coddie went on to earn a Doctorate in Theology, and is a fine minister in his own right.

Mikki was last located at a public convention center where she works day security. She is still married and has two children.

The Creole Queen still lives in Temple with her white "cowboy." I do hope she's happy.

The female that invited me to St. James is in her late forties and is becoming a tragic tale. She's showing signs of extreme mental stress brought on by advanced liver disease. I hear tell that she's still hoping that she and I will "hook up" before it's too late.

I'm open to suggestions on that matter because I just don't know. There's been a lot of water go under that bridge!

Cherry is still leading dialogues on racism and traveling around the country speaking. She's one very super special lady who lives the Dream daily. It was her patience and kindness that got me through some very tough spots while I was metamorphosing from the racist worm I used to be to this little butterfly that is spreading the word.

I returned to St. James briefly in 2004. The church had changed. It has gone high tech. Those golden colored letters aren't there anymore above the arch up front. I do hope Jesus Is Lord with all the strobe lights flashing!

The SBC church has grown to over 18,000 members with three campuses. I was offered a Pastoral Counseling position at one point, but it just didn't feel right. Maybe it's because there was a book in me to be written that might not have happened otherwise. I wish them the very best of everything and much love!

That Catholic Charismatic Church is growing by leaps and bounds. Imagine seeing a beautiful rainbow of people lifting their hands together in praise. There's just something about taking the Holy Eucharist. It seems to have a healing and soothing affect for me.

I attend meetings on the south side now and then. There's this thirties-something sister who thinks I'm sexy. Now ain't that a hoot!

Miss Irma and I still see each other two or three times a week. We go on dates now and then, or just sit and talk about the old times. We just "kicking it." She's still fiercely religious on Sundays and a character the rest of the week. She's the Benefactor of my Last Will and Testament. I couldn't think of anybody nicer to give what the Good Lord has given to me.

And me? Well, I had planned on semi-retiring in 2004 after going through a move from Pasadena back to Houston, Texas. I wanted to begin a new career of writing! In August of 2004, I had a massive heart attack resulting in quad-by-pass heart surgery. I'm fully retired today – except for this writing thing. Fate has a way of playing some very interesting tricks on us. Presently, I live exactly where I said I would never come back to in Texas! The apartment complex is what remains of the old Union Station in Houston. It was renovated and is home for several US veterans who are retired. I'm a very happy camper. My apartment is filled with none other than another N-scale model railroad. I keep telling folks that it's never too late to have a happy childhood! I'm at peace with God and myself. As far as I know, I don't have any enemies and a whole lot of friends.

Special Note: God gave me over 3000 "Spiritual children" in my days as a Licensed Chemical Dependency Counselor and Licensed Social Worker. The vast majority of those I served are staying clean and sober. Now that's a legacy I can live with!

By the way, how are you doing? My prayer is that you find what you are looking for. How about some peace and happiness? If you read the entire book, I do hope you find your Mammy also, or maybe, help some other white male who is looking. There are literally millions of Spiritual seeds that have been planted over the years. Water them with care and see just how fast they bloom into real Peace and Justice for all. Hey, isn't that what we all say we want? I'll let you be the judge on that one.

There are a couple of other things that I want to say, the reason I wrote this book is because I'm tired. I'm tired of seeing good people (on both sides) continue to live in fear and hurt each other. As Dr. King used to call them, my "sick white brothers" need a little help because many of them are beginning to see "what time it is." They getting older! My hope and prayer in writing this small book is to start a revolution – a new grass roots Civil Rights Movement. This "time" maybe all parties will actually talk to each other rather than shout at each other. Anybody know where a hammer is? We need to smash that screeching amplifier all to hell, then maybe we can actually hear each other communicate. That's my personal dream from my heart to all of yours.

Just one more thing please. Before I disappear at the end of this page, I want to express what many others should have said for so many years prior. So, here goes! First, I personally acknowledge my own part in the perpetuation of racism by just saying nothing for the most part. I did use the "N word" a few times while growing up, but that was back then. Acknowledgment is where justice begins which leads to peace eventually. Secondly, for all those times when I could have said something to stop hate, or evil words, and did or said nothing, I AM truly sorry. I mean that from the bottom of my heart to yours. Third, after acknowledgment and apology should come an offering of amends. That means I am willing to do my humble part to make up for my silence in the perpetuation of the madness. You have my word that I have not been silent, nor will I ever be silent again. I guess that's part of what this book is about as well. I'm doing my bit to start something that is actually attainable – a grass roots Civil Rights Movement where the load is shared equally for a change. I'd like to see folks come to the Table of Blessing and share not just the steak and potatoes, but a very delightful salad courtesy of a Loving God who sees us equally. There's this question in First John 4: 20 that goes something like this "…how can you say you love God whom you have not seen when you hate your brother whom you have?" I guess that pretty much sums up what time it really is, doesn't it? I love you! Now pass that on!

John Thomas Keating, MA

About the Author

John Thomas Keating is in his late fifties and a product of an America that should have never been. He witnessed racism, segregation and discrimination up close and personal. He saw - from a closet where he was hiding - the ominous glow of a cross burning in the family's front yard. He felt the pain of separation from the only love he received in his tender years. That security came in the form of a semi-literate common law wife of a black sharecropper in Southwestern Georgia. This child was special having been the object of shameful abuse, rejection and abandonment. Picture that child being exposed to hatred that surpassed human imagination! He grew into manhood to serve in the Air Force when the United States faced its first defeat in its history of conflict. He returned home to apathy. He failed in Bible College; failed at another university; and finally, failed himself with repeated abuse of alcohol, illicit drugs and seventeen years of marriage entered into for all the wrong reasons. He faced being flat-line dead due to overdose. He was told that he had a year to live in December of 1989 because of advanced liver disease. He entered treatment and took to the Twelve Steps of Recovery like a duck takes to water. His entire outlook upon life began to change. He went back to school and graduated from Houston Baptist University with a respectable 3.14 average. He actually made the National Dean's List for 1992! He went on to earn a Master of Arts Degree in Counseling from Prairie View A & M University partially financing his tuition on a Reverse Minority Scholarship!

Yes, he's white. He became a Licensed Social Worker and later on a Licensed Chemical Dependency Counselor. He had the courage to get a divorce and start life anew. He faced yet another diagnosis of advanced hepatitis in 1997 being given three to five years to live! He found himself as the Lead Counselor at the largest drug and alcohol treatment center in Houston right in the middle of "the hood." During that same time his imagination was sparked to find the love that gave him so very much when he was only six years old – his Mammy. He began his search after 42 years separation to say thank you for what she had so generously shared with him. He says he owes his global view to a Loving God and that very special lady who had every reason to hate, but chose not to! He'll tell you that gratitude will get you a long, long way in life. The love she gave him he passed on to over 2,500 men - primarily African Americans – who are staying "clean and sober." He'll tell you that is a legacy he can definitely live with. Not bad for a short, four-eyed white boy who wasn't supposed to live past the age two in the first place! A published author gave him very good advice when he decided to begin a writing career: "Write about what you know and nothing else." He followed that suggestion and this story is the result – an in depth look at racism up close and personal. He went into the "blackness" and was changed forever. He knows too much to return to the status of "white privilege." In spite of a massive heart attack in August of 2004 that left him almost penniless, he just keeps on "sucking air" and believing that the way things are do not have to remain. There is a better way if only people will just learn to "get along" and get real! The healing is in facing the pain of the present to find a much better future with justice and peace for all!